Creating a Beautiful
Water Garden

THE Complete Pond Builder

Helen Nash

Sterling Publishing Co., Inc.
New York

Designed by Judy Morgan

Library of Congress Cataloging-in-Publication Data

Nash, Helen, 1944–
    The complete pond builder : creating a beautiful water garden   /   by
Helen Nash.
        p.   cm.
    Includes index.
    ISBN 0-8069-3866-8
    1. Water gardens.   I. Title.
SB423.N36   1995
690′.89—dc20   95-40525
                                                                CIP

Credits

Page 3: designed by Jeffrey S. Butz; photographed by Walter Kuhn III; page 4:
designed and photographed by Robert Johnson; page 6: designed by the late Kiyoshi
Okuhara; photographed by H. Nash; page 8: courtesy of Gilbert Perennials;
photographed by Greg Speichert; page 20: designed and photographed by Joe B.
Dekker; page 42: designed and photographed by George Rosicky; photographed by
H. Nash; page 47: designed by Joe Scheidler; photographed by T. J. Smith; page 54:
designed and photographed by Cla Allgood; page 63: courtesy of Reimer
Waterscapes; page 71: photographed by Richard Schmitz; page 76: designed and
photographed by Eamonn Hughes; page 92: designed and photographed by Cla
Allgood; page 104: courtesy of Waterford Gardens; photographed by Greg Speichert;
page 114: courtesy of Florentine Craftsmen.

    Illustration on page 111 courtesy of Maryland Aquatic Nurseries. All other
illustrations by Marilyn Cook and Helen Nash.

1   3   5   7   9   10   8   6   4   2

First paperback edition published in 1996 by
Sterling Publishing Company, Inc.
387 Park Avenue South, New York, N.Y. 10016
© 1996 by Helen Nash
Distributed in Canada by Sterling Publishing
% Canadian Manda Group, One Atlantic Avenue, Suite 105
Toronto, Ontario, Canada M6K 3E7
Distributed in Great Britain and Europe by Cassell PLC
Wellington House, 125 Strand, London WC2R 0BB, England
Distributed in Australia by Capricorn Link (Australia) Pty Ltd.
P.O. Box 6651, Baulkham Hills, Business Centre, NSW 2153, Australia
Printed in Hong Kong
All rights reserved.

Sterling ISBN 0-8069-3866-8 Trade
0-8069-3867-6 Paper

For Ed Graves and T.J. Smith . . . and
"The Ponds of Cass County."

ACKNOWLEDGMENTS

This book would not have been possible without the kind sharing of information, tips, ponds, photographs, and support by many special individuals and companies.

The companies: Adams & Adkins, Bamboo Fencer, Charleston Aquatic Nurseries, Florentine Craftsmen, Kinsman Company, Mac-Court Ponds, Oly-Ola Super Edge, Plow & Hearth, RCI Sales & Marketing, Rena Corporation, Smith Kruger, Inc., The Stone Center, Indianapolis, Toscano, Walkmaker, Inc., Wastewater Engineering Professionals, Inc., and White Flower Farm Plantsmen. A special thanks to Joe Kalbas, Nancy Larson, and Fred Bell of Firestone Building Products Company, Richard Schuck and Kelly Billing of Maryland Aquatic Nurseries, Henry and Carole Reimer of Reimer Waterscapes, and Betty Bailey and Brian Bergeson of Seepage Control, Inc.

The pond builders: Cla Allgood of Allgood Outdoors in Cumming, Georgia; Scott Bates of Grass Roots Nursery in New Boston, Michigan; Jeffrey S. Butz of Landscapes Unlimited in Indianapolis, Indiana; Joe B. Dekker of The Waterscaping Company in Wycliff, New Jersey; Eamonn Hughes of Hughes Water Gardens in Tualatin, Oregon; Greg Jones of Waterfall Landscapes & Sunrooms in Chicago, Illinois; Dan Lunsford of Custom Fountains in Indianapolis, Indiana; Robert Johnson of Pond Care in Fresno, California; Greg Maxwell of Maxwell Tree Service in Ft. Wayne, Indiana; Post Landscape Services in Atlanta, Georgia; Clyde and Tina Riley of CCR Group in Indianapolis, Indiana; Joe and Lee Scheidler of Spring Creek Landscaping in Logansport, Indiana and Gary G. Wittstock of Aquascape Designs in Wheaton, Illinois.

The photographers: Gerry Abel, Kevin Carmean, Carol Christensen, Joe Cook, Roseanne Conrad, Lee Dreyfuss, Nancy Griego, Oliver Jackson, Walter Kuhn III, Bill Marocco, and Debbie Moak, with a special thanks to T.J. Smith, Greg Speichert, Perry D. Slocum and Gary G. Wittstock.

The pond owners: Marilyn Ahr, Judy Amor, Mr. and Mrs. Murney Aspden, David Bolles, Milton and Jean Cole, John and Gwen Cord, Gary and Paula Cosgray, T. DeGasperi, John and Marian Dressler, Tad Dill and Jane Dill, Nelson and Fran Fluker, Jack Graham, Guy and Sharon Henriksen, Mr. and Mrs. Francis Huyge, Lou and Lynn Jenkins, Jonathan and Faye Kellerman, Mr. and Mrs. Patrick Kelly, Bob and Mary Kerns, Hugh and Emmy Leeman, Kelly and Marty Leeman, Jim Martinson, Ed Millinger, Tom and Ilsa Morris, Fred Mueller, Mr. and Mrs. Don Newman, Dennie and the late Kiyoshi Okuhara, Paul Poulet, Wayne Reid and Bill Reid, George Rosicky, Ken and Donna Schenk, Richard and Linda Schmitz, Stan and Nancy Smith, Mr. and Mrs. Ward Smith, Clifford and Ruth Tallman, Bill and Kathy Vajdik, and the late Mrs. Fawnie Williams.

A special thanks, as always, to my dear friend and editor, Hannah Steinmetz, for pulling it all together, and to my cousin, Marcia Saatzer, for finding the talented Lee Dreyfuss.

CONTENTS

INTRODUCTION

Like The Pond Doctor, *this book was born of frustration: The frustration of following overly simple directions of pond installation only to have structural and design problems visit later with a vengeance; the frustration of having to pore over book after book searching for necessary information for a well-constructed, relatively repair-free pond; and the frustration of being so rank an amateur that the most I could count on was hitting my thumb instead of the nail head.*

Consequently, the vision of The Pond Builder *is from the perspective of a dreaming amateur who lacks the funds to hire a professional designer and builder but who wants more than just a hole in the ground with a rock necklace. From inception through writing,* The Pond Builder's *focus has been "What do I want to know?" You see, both my mother and my husband quite freely admit that the one word that best describes me is "klutz." Complicated directions and mathematics are not my forte. All I want are the facts in the clearest, simplest format possible—along with the insider tricks of the trade so what I do looks good and works well.*

Unquestionably, water features in a garden add a delightful and soothing dimension to the environment. My own philosophy is that home and yard should be a haven from the sometimes too rapidly changing world beyond. A yard may be one special place in the world to create timeless moments of magic. I hope The Pond Builder *is like a magic wand to make your secret dreams of beauty and tranquility come true.*

Helen Nash

Designed and photographed
by Cla Allgood

Chapter One

DESIGN DECISIONS

A meandering stream with bog plantings and a water garden create a magical world in the backyard.

Photo courtesy of Maryland Aquatic Nurseries

It is human nature to be attracted to water—creeks, streams, rivers, lakes, and oceans. Peaceful, soul-satisfying mysteries are inherent in the waters around us. And throughout our history, incorporating water into the immediate environment has been a time-honored practice. It is the stuff of dreams and magic.

As the modern world increases in complexity, the simple tranquility of water in the garden invites us to create tangible, serene moments. However, creating the delight of a water garden in the backyard takes a great deal more than a moment of serendipity. Meticulously thorough planning is probably the most important factor in the successful implementation of the dream of a water garden.

FIRST DECISIONS—LOOK AT IT OR LIVE WITH IT?

The notion of the backyard as an outdoor living space is not new. If we live in the yard—entertaining, playing, relaxing, or working—the parameters of that space are

A pond sited next to the patio can be enjoyed from both inside and outside the home.

Photo by Greg Jones

A pond nestled between the home and nearby woods integrates the pond within its setting.

Photo by T.J. Smith

significantly different from what they would be for someone merely sitting at a window and gazing outward. So, the first decision to be made in planning a water garden is: Is it for contemplation from a window or patio or will it be the center of outdoor activity?

Looking at It

If the water garden is primarily to be part of the scenic view, it must be located within an aesthetically pleasing vantage of the home's living areas. From the kitchen window, living room sofa, or picnic table on the deck, it must be as satisfying to view the pond and its reflections as it is at closer range.

Living with It

Living with the water garden means being concerned with many other factors in addition to overall view. The pond must be accessible—pathways to and around it, decking, paving, seating, perhaps even a gazebo, invite a more intimate experience of the garden's mysteries. Such a pond may not even be visible from within the house; it may present itself as a stunning surprise hidden in a remote corner of the yard, framed by its own cozy setting. However, unless a pond is specifically intended to be part of a private retreat area, visibility from the house and ease of access enhance its year-round enjoyment and should certainly be taken into account in the planning stages.

A lined, natural pond enhances the scenic vista from the home.

Photo by Richard Schmitz

A pond sited adjacent to a lower-level patio is also enjoyed from the upper-level deck.

Photo by T.J. Smith

A formal pond focuses both on geometric design and on the water itself.

Photo by H. Nash, courtesy of The Grand Hotel, Mackinac Island, Michigan

Tucked into delightful flower beds, a garden seat and pond invite quiet moments.

Photo courtesy of Reimer Waterscapes

TIP

A general guide for style planning: straight lines are formal; curved lines are informal.

WHAT STYLE TO BUILD?

While personal choices present some options in materials used, the basic style or design of the water garden is all but predetermined by the style of the home and the existing landscaping. For a water garden to have not only a professional look but also to have that comforting feeling of belonging, it must be in keeping with its surroundings. If a home is distinctly formal and the landscaping simple and geometric, so, too, should be the water garden.

On the other hand, if the home is a ranch style, for example, and the landscaping more casual, a free-form, informal pond is more suitable.

Finally, in an expansive yard, especially one enhanced with native trees and flowers, an informal, natural wildlife design would be appropriate.

PLANNING FOR SAFETY

Safety is the single most important factor in planning a water garden. No matter how beautifully constructed and landscaped, a water garden that invites accidents to unsuspecting visitors or children rapidly becomes a nightmare.

The accessibility of the pond is the most obvious safety factor to consider. Siting a pond off the edge of a deck can result in catastrophic falls by guests, especially children. Likewise, a bridge spanning a pond may invite sudden dunkings. In both cases, closely spaced, sturdy railings should be provided.

In urban neighborhoods, it is a good idea to surround the entire pond area (and, perhaps, the entire yard as well) with a fence to protect small children. It may even be necessary to keep the gate locked. Subdivision and city ordinances frequently have regulations concerning the construction of swimming pools and ponds. Check these carefully before undertaking any construction. Even though such ordinances may not specify water gardens, it is wise to ascertain the legal position of having such an "attractive nuisance" in the yard without appropriate safety protections. These same ordinances may also specify the distance from a property line a pool or pond may be constructed. Even though water garden construction may have slipped through the cracks and may not be specifi-

cally regulated, the legal repercussions in the unfortunate event of an accident may be comparable to those for a swimming pool. Homeowner insurance policies, too, may have stipulations to be satisfied.

If safety and legal considerations make a water garden too fraught with problems, other water features can be considered. (See Chapter 11.)

Electricity is a vital safety concern. Most water gardens use an electrically powered recirculation pump. Outdoor extension cords lying about on the ground can be very dangerous. The safest and best way to deal with electricity around a water garden is to have the service line buried underground up to a point near the pond. Even then, it should be connected via a contact circuit breaker designed to prevent fatal shocking. In the interest of safety, all electrical work should be performed by a licensed professional.

Although lined, this Eamonn Hughes informal pond recreates a natural setting.
Photo by E. Hughes

Young children are reminded to stay away from the pond with an inconspicuous fence of predator netting.
Photo by Lee Dreyfuss

Another safety factor to consider is water depth, especially around the edges of the pond. Plan a foot-deep shelf or ledge around the edge of the pond to provide ease of exit. Make this shelf 18 to 36 inches wide to provide a safe footing.

THE PURPOSE OF A WATER GARDEN OR POND

Safety considerations may help determine the purpose of the water garden or pond. Should legitimate safety concerns make a four or five-foot-deep pond too costly, plans for a pond that includes koi may have to be altered to accommodate goldfish, which do not require such depths.

Formal ponds may feature fountains, precluding the addition of water lilies. Formal ponds need not be planted at all, while informal ones may incorporate a variety of aquatic plants that need varying depths for optimal growth.

to soften the sharpness of the elevation. And while siting the pond at the lowest elevation on the property may look natural because this is where water usually collects, pond flooding and possible contamination from rain run-offs are likely problems. Should such a site be the only available choice, construction plans should include drainage provisions. Good drainage is necessary to prevent the liner from bubbling up due to ground water pressure.

If the site is sloped, plan for terracing in a formal pond, and for possible terracing or water courses or waterfalls to take advantage of the elevation changes in an informal pond. Soil from the pond excavation can be used at the lower end to level the actual pond site, which must be wholly level to avoid uneven distances between

Koi ponds may require special filtration and design considerations.
Photo by Lee Dreyfuss

> ### TIP
> *Plan water-garden depths of 18 to 36 inches for water lilies and 1 to 4 inches over the pot tops of marginal aquatics.*

SITE SELECTION

The style and purpose of the water garden determines, to some extent, the actual siting of the pond. Formal ponds, for example, must be sited to fit into the balance of symmetrical features and structures in the existing landscape.

Similarly, the pond constructed as a water garden should be sited to receive maximum sunlight. While a formal pond can be sited in the shade, where it can feature a fountain, less than three to five hours of available sunlight seriously limits planting options in the informal pond.

The lay of the land is an important consideration in order to avoid major excavation and restructuring of the entire yard. Obviously, a pond sited at the top of a ridge would look unnatural, although spoil, or the dirt from the excavation, can be used

A small koi pond is tucked between two apartment buildings.
Photo by H. Nash

A small entryway pond proves inviting to visitors.

Photo by Eamonn Hughes

the water and the pond edges. While it is especially important with sloping land to precheck the level of the proposed site for the pond, ground that appears level may have slight variances of an inch or two that will mar the pond's final appearance.

A large, informal pond captures reflections of the sky and the imagination of the viewer.

Photo by T.J. Smith

A sloped site is turned to good advantage for a pond next to the house.

Photo by Greg Jones

TIP

If it is necessary to build up a portion of the ground, the new soil should be well compacted to prevent settling. Add clay to give extra support to looser soils.

It may be necessary to dig a sample hole in the area under consideration to determine the water table. Ideally, this is done during the winter to assess the amount of ground water and its level in the sample excavation. In general, heavier, clay-concentrated soils hold more water and present more of a potential drainage problem. In such areas, drainage may have to be provided around the entire perimeter of a pond. Concrete constructions also may have to accommodate additional water pressure by being of increased thicknesses with appropriate reinforcements.

Avoid siting ponds near trees. Tree roots can invade the pond area and result in costly repairs later. Some trees, such as laburnum, holly, and yew are toxic. Pine needles, oaks, and maples produce tannic acid in water that is toxic to fish. Also, siting a pond downwind from deciduous trees is likely to result in additional autumn maintenance to keep leaves from collecting in the pond.

Windy sites limit the type of fountain that can be used in formal ponds because wind dissipates fine sprays and disrupts

their visual patterns. Aquatics, such as water lilies, are not happy in disrupted sites, and taller aquatics may be blown over and dirty the water with their soil. If such sites are unavoidable, plant windbreaks askew of prevailing winds to prevent downdrafts that disrupt the pond and deposit debris in it. Planted windbreaks are more effective in dissipating wind strength than solid structures, such as fences or buildings.

Setting a pond within decking offers accessibility and easy maintenance.

Photo courtesy of Reimer Waterscapes

TIP
For maximum sheltering effects, plant windbreaks up to ten times as far away from the pond as their height.

A small backyard can include more than one pond.

Photo by Oliver Jackson

Concrete and stone create ponds of great beauty and tranquility.

Photo by Deb Moak

TIP
Many professionals provide a liner under concrete construction.

PLANNING TO INTEGRATE THE POND INTO THE YARD

To integrate a formal pond into an existing yard, the rule of thumb is: Keep it simple and keep it geometrically symmetrical. Keep background plantings uncluttered. Quite often, formal ponds are set within an appropriately shaped paved area. Canal-type ponds may be set within a broad expanse of well-manicured lawn. Well-trimmed boxwood and classically styled planting urns and statuary can also integrate a formal pond into its surroundings.

Informal ponds can be integrated with their surroundings in a multitude of ways; flower beds, winding pathways, meandering streams, bog gardens, rock gardens, gazebos, decking, pebbles and rocks, mulching, bridges, paved entertainment areas, benches, planting containers, statuary, and railroad ties can all be enlisted, so

long as they fit in with the rest of the yard. Ironically, integrating an informal pond within its environment can be a more expensive and time-consuming project than a formal pond. This is probably because the task is performed in stages, thereby allowing a longer time period for the labor of love pond construction often becomes!

SELECTING A CONSTRUCTION METHOD

In spite of the fact that formal ponds are usually thought of in terms of concrete construction, they are easily made using liner construction methods. If concrete construction is the desired option, bear in mind that in some ways it is a more difficult method for the amateur. This does not mean that it is an impossible option. However, the amateur should confine his efforts to smaller ponds that are capable of being

Lined ponds can be adapted to various styles such as this small pond and water courseway.

Photo by T.J. Smith

built within one day and be totally familiar with the entire concrete procedure before starting a project.

With the development of EPDM, a synthetic rubber, liner construction has become not only relatively easy, but also long-lived. Other liner materials are available, but may not offer so long a life and may be susceptible to UV damage by the sun as well as to puncturing or to stress holes from stretching. Likewise, even a double layer of the heavier grades of plastic weed-barriers will need replacement in just a few years. What might initially appear an inexpensive material to use could eventually become most expensive when it has to be soon replaced.

Be certain that whatever material is used to line the pond is non-toxic to both fish and plants.

Ponds constructed in colder climates may need to have a layer of insulation, such as Styrofoam sheeting, between the pond membrane and the soil. The bottoms of these ponds should *not* be insulated as that would block geothermal heat and allow the pond to freeze solid.

TIP

Swimming pool liners and roofing materials may be chemically treated. These treatments are toxic to fish and plants.

Liner construction is especially useful for informal ponds.

Photo courtesy of Slocum Water Gardens

Chapter Two
POND CONSTRUCTION BASICS

FINDING AND MAINTAINING LEVELS

Water is always level, regardless of the lay of the land. Unless care is taken to establish an even grade for the pond edge all around, the pond will look lopsided. Most water gardens can be leveled with a builder's spirit level and a straightedge. A spirit level is a straightedge housing that encloses a bubble within a liquid. When the level is correct, the bubble will be centered. The bubble settles to the left or right depending on whether the grade is too high or too low. A straightedge is simply a long, straight, and smooth piece of lumber. While the spirit level can be used directly on the ground, resting it on a straightedge that is set across two stakes makes it possible to determine whether greater distances created by the length of the straightedge are level.

The approximate size and location of a pond can be marked with a string, rope, or hose. Remove the sod in strips with 2–3 inches of rooted soil so it can be used elsewhere. Stack the sod in a shady place and keep it moistened. The actual pond shape is then marked on the soil with spray paint or builder's chalk.

A carpenter's spirit level shows if both sides of the excavation are at the same level.

Photo courtesy of Maryland Aquatic Nurseries

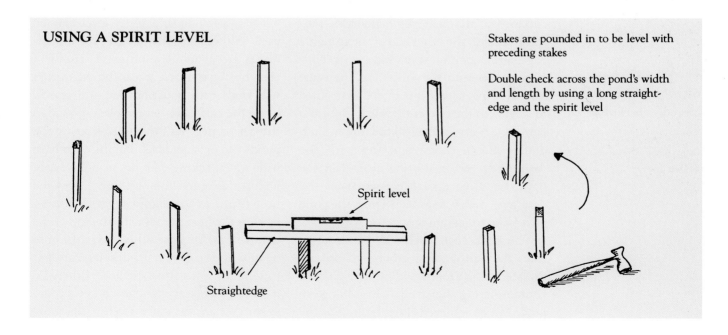

USING A SPIRIT LEVEL

Stakes are pounded in to be level with preceding stakes

Double check across the pond's width and length by using a long straightedge and the spirit level

Spirit level

Straightedge

Stakes, pointed on one end, are tapped into the ground 6 to 12 inches behind the pond's edge. The first stake is designated the *datum peg*, the guide which all of the others will be made to agree with. The top of the datum peg will reflect the pond's upper edge or the anticipated water level. Using the straightedge rested on top of the datum peg, the next peg is pounded into the ground so the other end of the straightedge rests upon its top, indicating both pegs are set into the ground at the same level. The next stake is pounded in to agree in level with the one just leveled. Once the pegs have been set level all the way around, double-check them, starting with the datum peg and measuring around in the opposite direction. Measure from the datum peg to leveled stakes across the pond area for extra assurance.

The pond edge levels may be set *higher* than the surrounding ground to prevent surface runoff from flooding and possibly contaminating the pond. This change in grade can be achieved either by grading the immediate surrounds of the pond or by using dirt from the excavation to build up the pond's area. In rainy regions it is a good idea to have the pond's edge four inches higher than the surrounding grade. If the pond edges will be built up, the soil should be very well tamped before the stakes are measured into it.

For larger ponds, a water level may be used. Although sophisticated hose attachments are available, sufficient length of clear hosing to reach across the excavation will work with a datum peg and stakes. Once the turf has been removed, pound in the datum peg, its top edge reflecting the pond's rim or water level. Fill the clear hose with water, taking care no air bubbles are within the water line. Tie one end of the hose firmly to the datum peg so the water level in the hose agrees with the top of the datum peg. Bring the other end of the hose up next to the datum peg, taking care not to spill any water from the hose, otherwise it will be necessary to start the procedure again. When the water level in the loose end of the hose agrees with the datum end, mark the water level on the loose end with tape or a laundry pen. Then carefully take the hose to each stake around the pond's perimeter. Pound the stakes in until their top edges and the water in the hose agree with the marked level.

A professional excavator will probably use a telescopic apparatus that requires the assistance of a second person. Laser levels can be operated by only one person. These levels are beneficial in determining level heights of large waterfall designs, as well as determining even distribution of gravel or sand layers within the excavation when it is important to maintain specific depths.

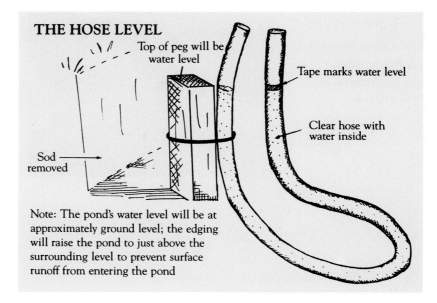

THE HOSE LEVEL

Top of peg will be water level

Tape marks water level

Clear hose with water inside

Sod removed

Note: The pond's water level will be at approximately ground level; the edging will raise the pond to just above the surrounding level to prevent surface runoff from entering the pond

USING A HOSE LEVEL

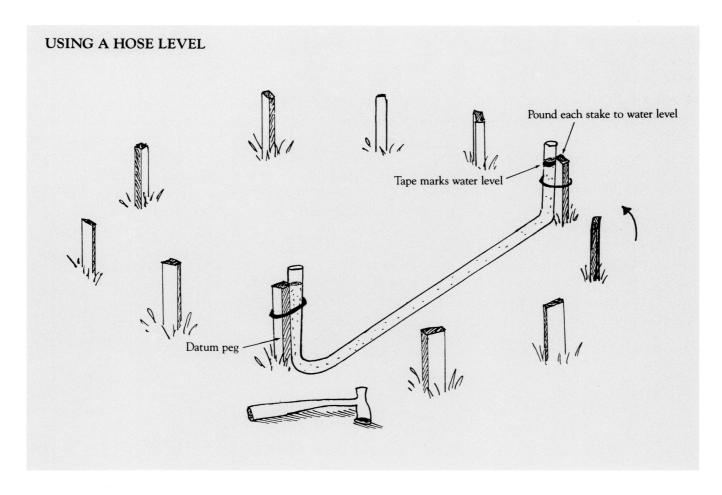

Pound each stake to water level

Tape marks water level

Datum peg

Spray paint marks the excavation site.

Photo courtesy of Firestone Building Products

EXCAVATION

Smaller water gardens can be excavated by hand. Remove one shovel's depth at a time from the entire pond area. (To ease the cleanup job, have tarps nearby and put the topsoil and subsoil on them.) If a shelf is to be constructed within the pond, mark the edge around the excavation once the desired depth has been attained. The shelf's

EXCAVATING THE POND

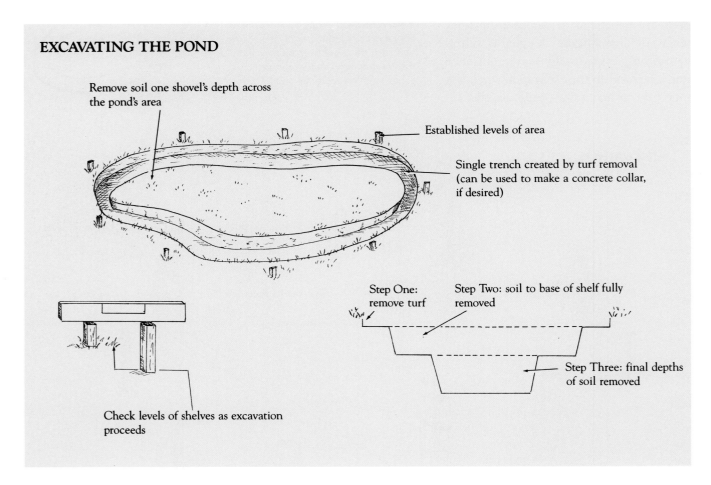

Remove soil one shovel's depth across the pond's area

Established levels of area

Single trench created by turf removal (can be used to make a concrete collar, if desired)

Check levels of shelves as excavation proceeds

Step One: remove turf

Step Two: soil to base of shelf fully removed

Step Three: final depths of soil removed

EXCAVATING A LOW-LYING AREA

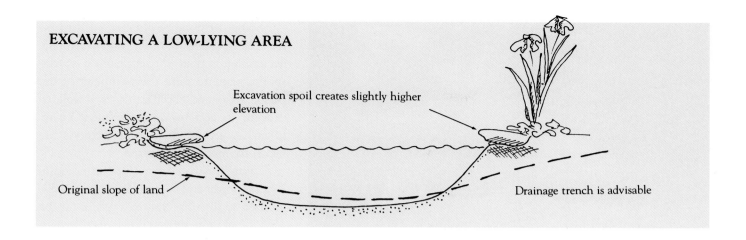

Excavation spoil creates slightly higher elevation

Original slope of land

Drainage trench is advisable

EXCAVATING A SLOPE

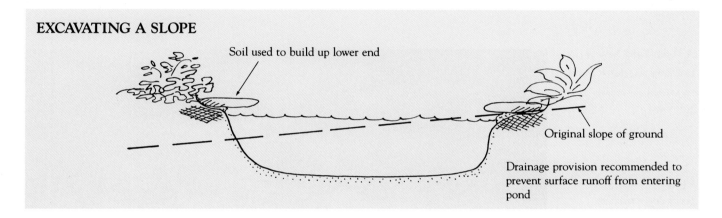

Soil used to build up lower end

Original slope of ground

Drainage provision recommended to prevent surface runoff from entering pond

width should be at least 12 inches, although 18 inches or more will allow extra stability as well as enough space if wall reinforcements must be used. The excavation proceeds in the same manner to the pond bottom.

Except for construction of larger natural ponds with gently sloped sides, most ponds should have nearly vertical sides, at least from the shelf to the top edge. This allows pond edging to be constructed with a minimum amount of visible pond wall. A slight slope in the wall can appear a definite bulge in the finished pond. Keeping the sides nearly vertical from the shelf down to the pond bottom makes for a more accessible pond. Imagine trying to walk uphill on wet, slippery material; distinct, fairly level "steps" are safer and easier to use.

Excavate the very bottom of the pond with a slope to a deeper sump area, usually at one end of the pond, for draining the pond by a submersible pump. This simple construction precludes the need for complicated bottom drains.

Be sure, also, that the depth takes into account any gravel or sand layers to be beneath the pond's membrane. At the pond's upper edge, which has already been established as perfectly level, creating an area just slightly below grade will allow for pond overflow during heavy rains.

Should the pond be planned for the lowest area in the yard where water normally accumulates, plan the excavation so the spoil is used to raise the perimeter of the pond. Tamp and compact this soil well, to prevent its settling in subsequent years. Likewise, ensure drainage provisions beneath the pond's membrane.

A pond excavated on a slope will require that the lower end be built up. Again, well-tamped spoil from the excavation can be used. Generally, subsoil is more stable than topsoil. It may be necessary to incorporate soil reinforcement such as clay.

A steep bank seems an unlikely site for a pond.

Photo courtesy of Reimer Waterscapes

Proper excavation and pond construction transform sloped property.

Photo courtesy of Reimer Waterscapes

DRAINAGE

In areas with a high water table, pay special attention to drainage of ground water that might push the pond's membrane up from the ground. Generally, several inches of crushed stone placed over the entire pond bottom will suffice. Two or three inches of sand is placed over this.

In cases of a very high water table, it may be necessary to install drainage trenches across the bottom of the pond excavation. These trenches can be plugged into a perimeter drainage system that takes the water away from the pond area.

Such drainage trenches may also be advisable if surface runoff presents a problem. The trench is dug between the runoff source and the pond to intercept and redirect the water.

In either case, a trench is dug to the necessary depth with a one-inch-per-ten-feet drop in depth as the trench proceeds to the new drainage area. (This may be an existing ditch, a constructed sump area, or a round-about return to the original drainage direction on the other side of the pond.) Line the entire trench with a geotextile fabric that allows water passage without admitting soil, if desired. A perforated PVC pipe is placed in the bottom of the trench and the trench is filled with crushed stone to within an inch or so of the ground's surface. The trench may then be camouflaged with mulch, plantings, or sod.

A drainage tile set at the pond bottom will prevent the liner from bubbling up in high water table areas.

Photo courtesy of Firestone Building Products

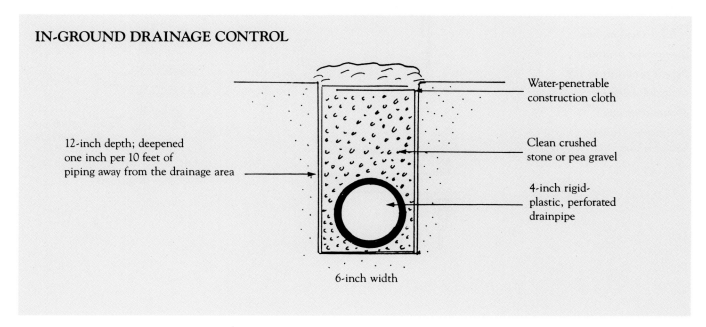

IN-GROUND DRAINAGE CONTROL

12-inch depth; deepened one inch per 10 feet of piping away from the drainage area

Water-penetrable construction cloth

Clean crushed stone or pea gravel

4-inch rigid-plastic, perforated drainpipe

6-inch width

A drainage trench dug to the pond's depth may be necessary to divert ground water from the pond.

Photo courtesy of Firestone Building Products

A laser level makes certain the drainage trench proceeds at the required depths to ensure drainage.

Photo courtesy of Firestone Building Products

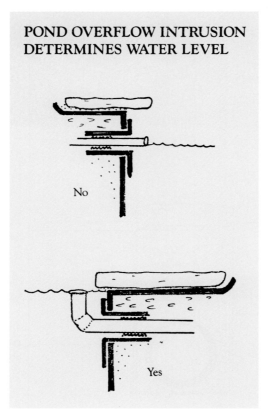

POND OVERFLOW INTRUSION DETERMINES WATER LEVEL

No

Yes

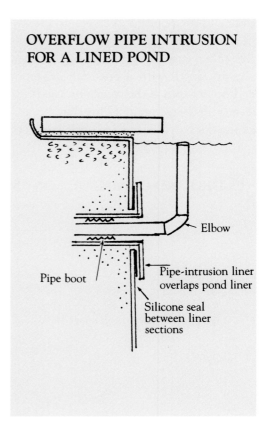

OVERFLOW PIPE INTRUSION FOR A LINED POND

Elbow

Pipe-intrusion liner overlaps pond liner

Pipe boot

Silicone seal between liner sections

POND OVERFLOW WITH LINEUPS™

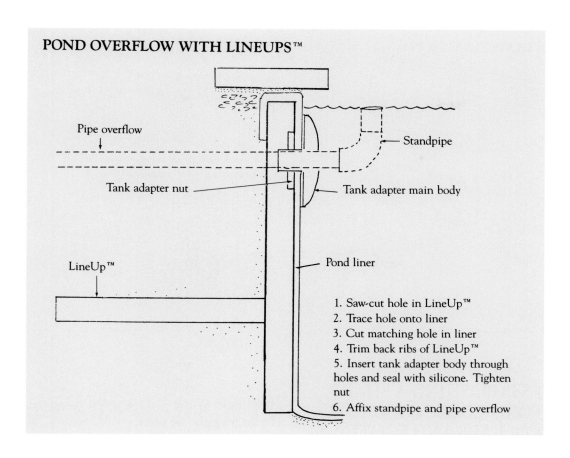

Pipe overflow

Standpipe

Tank adapter nut

Tank adapter main body

LineUp™

Pond liner

1. Saw-cut hole in LineUp™
2. Trace hole onto liner
3. Cut matching hole in liner
4. Trim back ribs of LineUp™
5. Insert tank adapter body through holes and seal with silicone. Tighten nut
6. Affix standpipe and pipe overflow

SIMPLE EARTH POND OVERFLOW

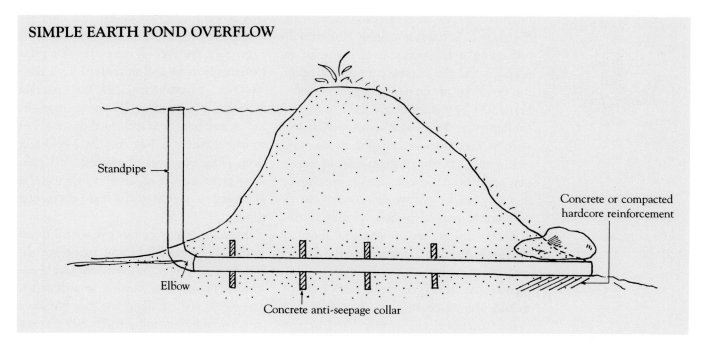

Standpipe

Concrete or compacted hardcore reinforcement

Elbow

Concrete anti-seepage collar

CONCRETE COLLAR CONSTRUCTION

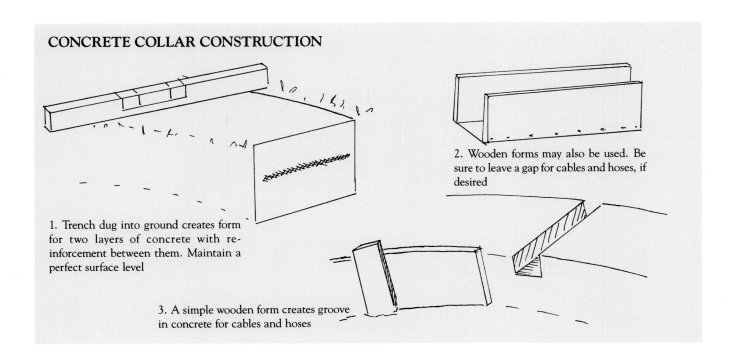

1. Trench dug into ground creates form for two layers of concrete with reinforcement between them. Maintain a perfect surface level

2. Wooden forms may also be used. Be sure to leave a gap for cables and hoses, if desired

3. A simple wooden form creates groove in concrete for cables and hoses

ESTABLISHING A SHARP POND EDGE: CONCRETE COLLARS AND FOOTINGS

A sharp pond edge is especially critical in lined ponds that are commonly edged with flat stones. Whatever edging is used will rest upon a flat surface. If the edge is rounded and the coping cannot rest upon the very edge of the pond, the pond membrane will be visible. Since the UV rays of sunlight can deteriorate some liner materials, protect the membrane from the sun.

It is easy to create a sharp edge in heavy clay soils, however, not all soils are clayey, and clay cracks in very dry conditions. A commonly recommended remedy is the concrete collar. In its simplest form, a steep-sided trench is dug around the perimeter before excavating the pond. This trench, which acts as the collar's form or mould, should be at least a foot wide and several inches deep, as mandated by any frost zone in the soil. Wooden or plastic forms may also be used.

Pour the concrete in two equal applications. Pour and tamp the first layer. Place wire screening or rebars over the layer inside a boundary of an inch of the concrete's edge. Pour the second layer over this reinforcement; tamp and smooth it. This construction, which is used also for concrete footings, is very effective in warmer climates, but may be impractical in zone 5 or 6, where the frost line may be 2 or 3 feet deep. The concrete, however, will gain some protection from ground-heaving if it is poured on a substantial layer of crushed stone.

Even so, it may be more practical to use concrete or cinder blocks to create the pond edge. The pond's shelf should be excavated of sufficient width to accommodate the block wall. Embedding the blocks in concrete may provide extra stability, as will

<table>
<tr><td>

TIP

Carole Reimer cautions that pea gravel does not make a good foundation for concrete. Its rounded edges will move in time, unlike the sharp edges of crushed stone that tend to knit together.

</td></tr>
</table>

filling the block hollows with concrete. Since the blocks are only eight inches high, an additional row of half-blocks, solid pavers, or solid engineering bricks may be necessary.

If heavy clay soil is readily available, it may be shaped and well tamped to create the necessary sharp, vertical edge. Stabilize soil that is built up around a pond by adding 6 to 8 ounces of dry cement per shovel of dirt.

Concrete blocks may be used to create firm, sharp edges for the pond.

Photo by Oliver Jackson

BOG GARDEN OVERFLOW FOR LINED POND

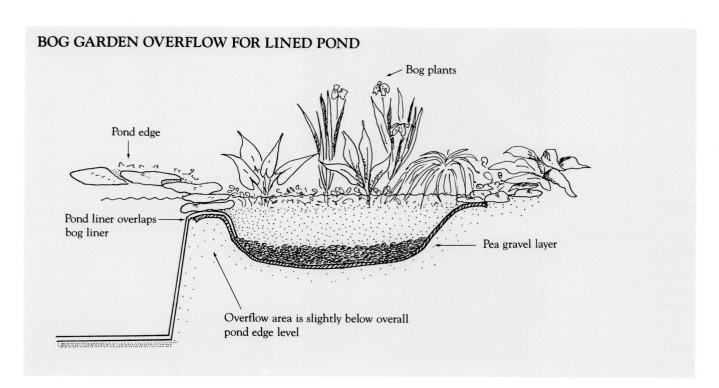

Bog plants

Pond edge

Pond liner overlaps bog liner

Overflow area is slightly below overall pond edge level

Pea gravel layer

Anchors are pounded into the pond perimeter at a carefully checked level.

The pond edge guide is fixed to the anchors.

The excavation is ready for lining.

Photos of Oly-Ola Super Edge courtesy of Maryland Aquatic Nurseries

ESTABLISHING A SHARP EDGE: LINEUP™ CONSTRUCTION

LineUps™ were developed by Dave Smith of Serenity Pond and Streams in Seal Beach, California, to solve problems with creating vertical, load-bearing walls in ponds. Each Lineup™ consists of a vertical, impermeable plate, 18″ high × 16″ wide, and a ribbed horizontal beam, 18″ × 16″, open to allow passage of moisture and roots. The molded HDPE material is ¼″, with 1½″ rib-reinforced pieces. LineUps™ are especially useful for pond-edge areas that must support heavy rocks or for areas that must be built up to grade.

To install, dig the pond edge in steps; first dig down vertically 13″. Leave an 18″ shelf that drops vertically another 5 inches. The first LineUp™ establishes the level grade by which successive installations are levelled. Using sand or soil, backfill behind the LineUp™ through the ribs of the horizontal beam until the unit is stabilized. Leave enough space at the top of the backfilling for about nine inches of liner to be overlapped and held in place by the remainder of the backfilling. In areas of heavy edge loads, reinforce the backfilling with "soil cement"—eight ounces of dry, powdered, portland cement mixed into four shovelfuls of soil, in a ratio of 30:1. Natural soil moisture will set the concrete within the soil.

STRAIGHT-SIDED CONSTRUCTION WITH LINEUPS™

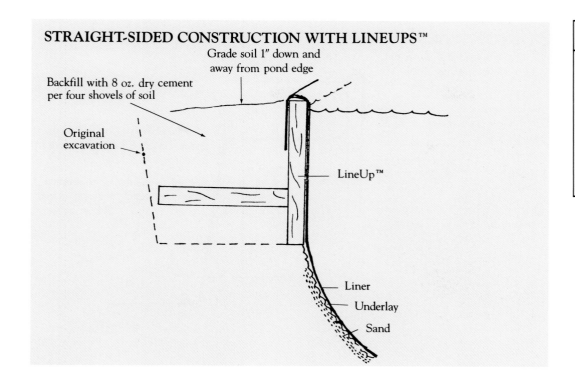

Grade soil 1″ down and away from pond edge

Backfill with 8 oz. dry cement per four shovels of soil

Original excavation

LineUp™

Liner

Underlay

Sand

TIP
In mixing "soil cement" into the pond excavation, be sure any organic matter has been removed from the soil.

LINEUP™ SOIL-ANCHORING SYSTEM

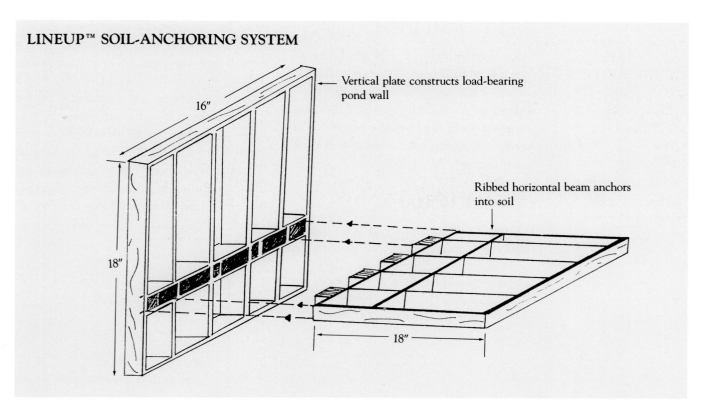

Vertical plate constructs load-bearing pond wall

16″

18″

Ribbed horizontal beam anchors into soil

18″

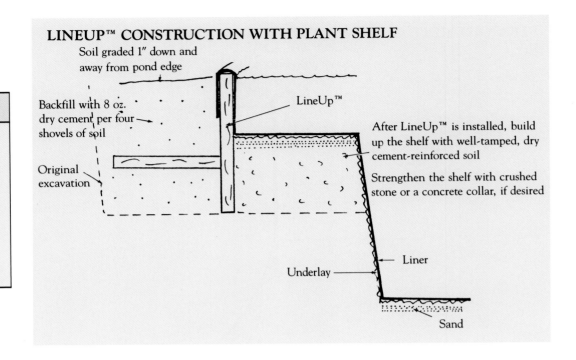

LINEUP™ CONSTRUCTION WITH PLANT SHELF

Soil graded 1″ down and away from pond edge

Backfill with 8 oz. dry cement per four shovels of soil

Original excavation

LineUp™

After LineUp™ is installed, build up the shelf with well-tamped, dry cement-reinforced soil

Strengthen the shelf with crushed stone or a concrete collar, if desired

Liner

Underlay

Sand

USING LINEUPS™ FOR INLET/OUTLET FITTINGS

Cut a hole into the plate of the LineUp™ with a hole drill or wood saw. Fit the liner over the LineUp™ and cut a matching hole through it for the fitting. Coat the liner, front and back, with single-component silicone and clamp it into place with bulkhead fittings.

CONCRETE HAUNCHES

For ponds that are edged with pebble beaches, planted areas, bog gardens, or turf, concrete haunches help firm the pond edge and preserve the water level. A concrete haunch is triangularly shaped with a broad base tapering up to a narrow top edge. The pond liner is carried over it and then dipped back down into the soil for camouflaging. If a haunch must be too large to be constructed free-form, form it by double-planking short strips of lumber. The haunches need not be of one piece; they need only be close enough together that the pond membrane does not dip between them, creating potential leaks.

MOVING HEAVY ROCKS

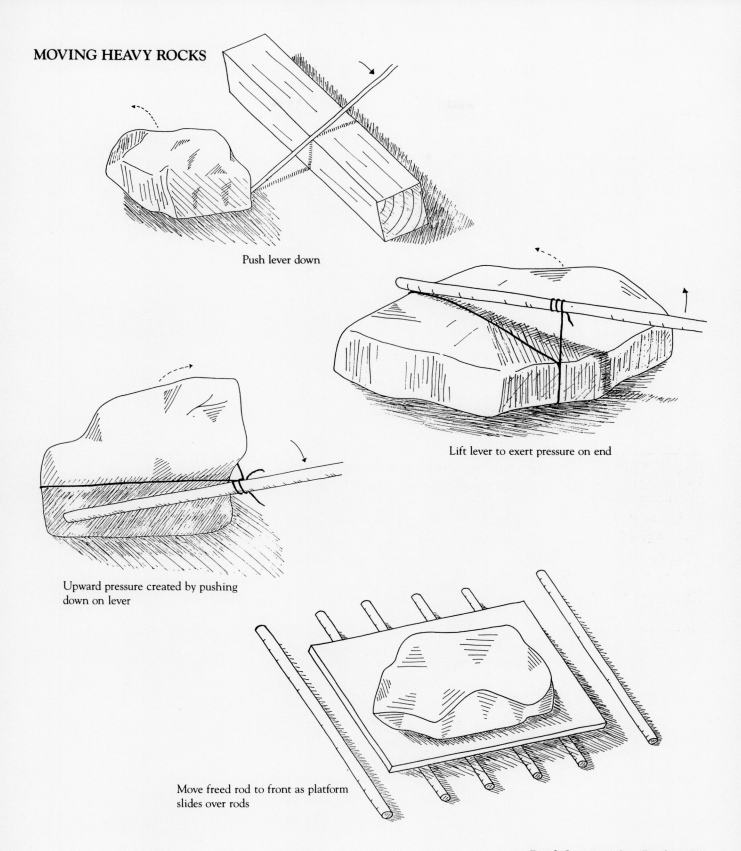

Push lever down

Lift lever to exert pressure on end

Upward pressure created by pushing
down on lever

Move freed rod to front as platform
slides over rods

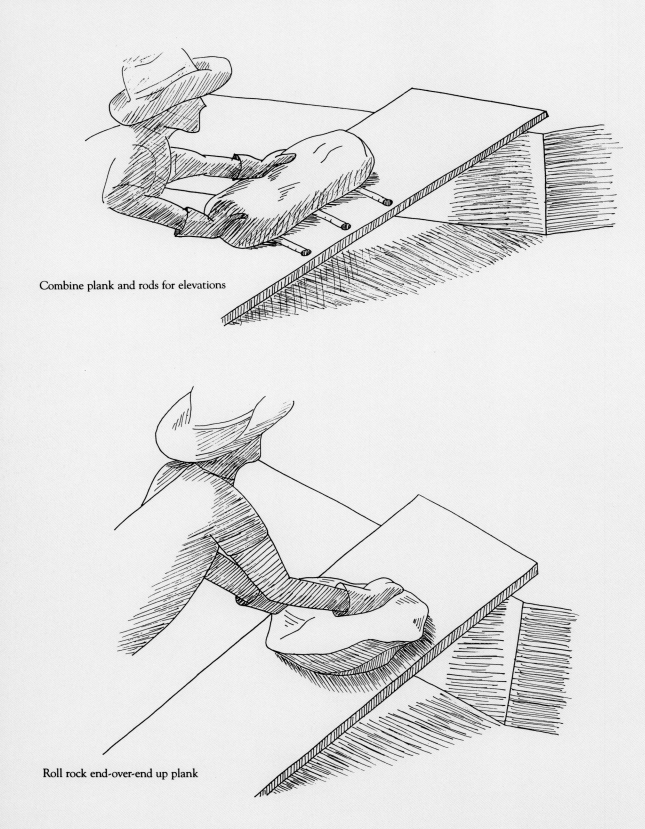

Combine plank and rods for elevations

Roll rock end-over-end up plank

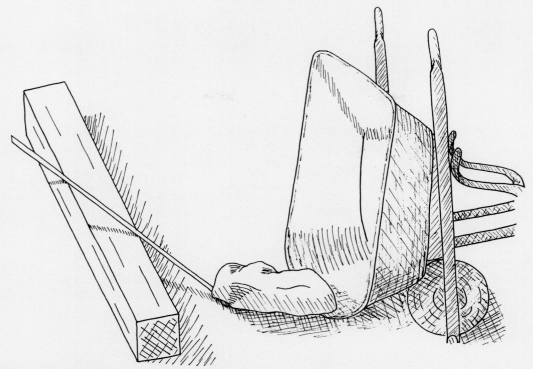

Leverage rock into wheelbarrow

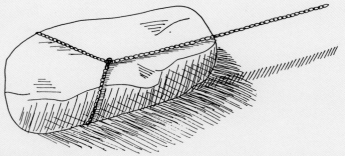

Chain or heavy rope pulls rock from above . . .

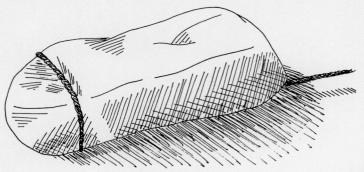

. . . or below

CUTTING FLAGSTONE

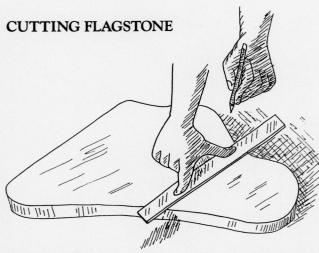

1. Rest the flagstone on a stable surface and mark a cutting line on both sides

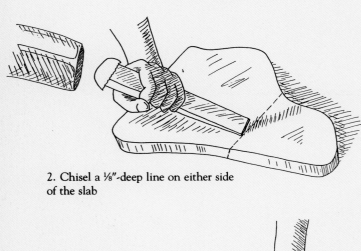

2. Chisel a ⅛"-deep line on either side of the slab

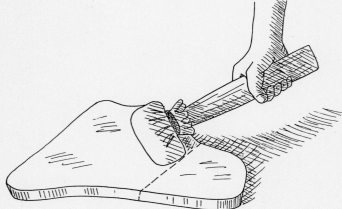

3. Muffled, heavy hammer strikes along the chiselled line

CUTTING FIELDSTONE

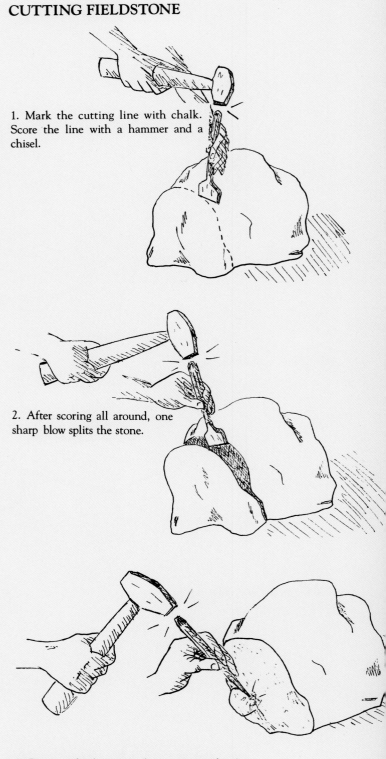

1. Mark the cutting line with chalk. Score the line with a hammer and a chisel.

2. After scoring all around, one sharp blow splits the stone.

3. Remove the bumps with a pointing chisel.

CUTTING BRICKS

1. A sharp blow with a trowel cuts some bricks.

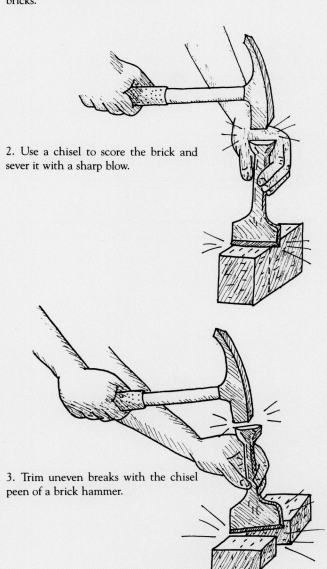

2. Use a chisel to score the brick and sever it with a sharp blow.

3. Trim uneven breaks with the chisel peen of a brick hammer.

BRICK WALL CONSTRUCTION

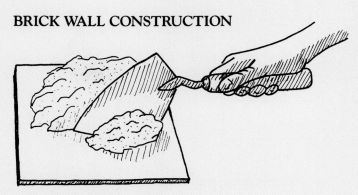

1. Cut mortar from mortar board. .

2. Pick up mortar with a snapping motion.

3. Use a sweeping motion to throw mortar onto bricks and spread it evenly.

4. Cut excess mortar from edges.

6. Butter brick end with sharp downward motion.

5. Lightly furrow center of mortar.

7. Shove brick into position to force out excess mortar.

CONCRETE FORM CONSTRUCTION

1.

Pour and tamp concrete into the plastic form.

2.

Smooth the concrete in the form and allow it to set firm.

3.

Remove the plastic form.

4.

Repeat the pouring to complete the desired area.

Photos courtesy of Walkmaster Company

Chapter Three
PREFORMED PONDS

Preformed ponds, usually made of strong plastic such as ABS, Acrylonitrile Butadiene Styrene polypropylene or HDP, high-density polythene, or fiberglass, are commonly available and easy to install. Although some are as large as twelve feet across, most are smaller, usually three to six feet across and 18 inches in depth. The very smallest are commonly only 12 inches deep. Being so shallow as well as so small, they may encounter problems with fluctuating water temperatures (which can stress fish) and with limited surface area (seriously limiting oxygen available for fish). It is very important with small preformed ponds to keep the number of fish lower than the normally recommended maximum stocking rate.

Plastic compositions cost less than fiberglass-reinforced or fiberglass constructions, but will not last as long. They may turn brittle, cracking and deteriorating within a few years. Even though the pond itself may be under warranty, the prospect

of labor and the expense of dismantling and replacing the pond after only a few years may offset the greater cost of a stronger pond form.

Another factor to consider when selecting a preformed pond is the strength of the top edge. Because heavy rocks or paving that rest on a plastic edging may buckle and crack the side walls of the pond, reinforcing the top edge may be a good idea. A concrete foundation, as well, may be wise. (See Chapter 2 for construction of these reinforcements.) Fiberglass generally will not require such reinforcement, although it may still be desirable, to provide pond-edge stability. To avoid frustration and unnecessary expense if a plastic pond is chosen, be sure the top edge is level and not warped.

Preformed ponds are available in a variety of standard forms. Many offer planting shelves. In selecting one of these ponds, be certain the shelf is wide enough for a potted plant. Surprisingly, many such shelves are too narrow to be functional. Fiberglass ponds, though more expensive, can be designed and constructed to specification, thereby offering the opportunity for relatively simple installation and individually creative design.

Two preformed ponds appear to be one large pond with a bridge crossover.

Photo courtesy of MacCourt Ponds

TIP

Fiberglass ponds without resin laminate on their undersides can be damaged by the lime in cement. Protect ponds installed over concrete with a layer of resin gelcoat.

Fiberglass preformed constructions are available in both pond and courseway forms.

Photo by Oliver Jackson, courtesy of Custom Fountains

TIP

An underlayer of flat stones on adequately reinforced ground stabilizes rock edging around a plastic pond.

TIP

To keep the sand on shelf excavations from sliding down into lower levels, keep it moist until the pond is set into the excavation.

TIP

Pond excavations can be marked on the soil with spray paint, builder's chalk, flour, cat litter, or sand.

BASIC INSTALLATION OF A PREFORMED POND

A professional preformed installation involves more than simply outlining the pond, digging the hole, and backfilling around the pond. In the first place, the edge of the pond should be an inch or two *above* the surrounding ground to avoid surface run-off entering the pond and possibly contaminating or flooding the pond. Two inches of sand should be placed in the bottom of the excavation, as well as on the surface of shelf excavations. This requires a decision prior to excavation: should the excavation be dug an extra amount for the sand cushion, or should it be dug to fit the actual pond shell, in which case the sand will elevate the pond above the surrounding ground? If the latter, the ground base for the pond edging will already be firm; an underlayer of crushed stone or flat supporting rocks can easily be used to support the pond edging. Place dirt from the excavation or fresh topsoil in the surrounding area to camouflage the slightly raised elevation of the pond. If the pond will be installed in a turfed area, remove sod in 6 to 8 inch-wide strips to simplify ground-marking.

Before any excavation is begun, set the preformed pond in its proposed location and *check the ground levels for the entire*

excavation. The job is considerably easier if the site is already fully level, but this may not always be. It is always wise to mark the levels with stakes before commencing any digging. Should the site present variations in level, monitor these guides throughout the excavation. (See Chapter 2.) A common option to correct level gradations is to use dirt from the pond excavation to build up the portion of the perimeter that is not level. Blend any accommodations into the surrounding ground to achieve a natural appearance and tamp firmly to avoid settling and loss of the level. (See Chapter 2 for soil reinforcement methods.)

A symmetrically shaped pond can be marked with the preformed pond lying upside down on the site. Set an irregularly shaped pond on the site with a weighted string hung over the edge as a guide for marking the ground. Excavate a shovel's depth at a time across the entire outlined form. Compare the depth of any planting shelves with the shovel depth. Excavate the

A limestone rubble edge incorporates a waterfall to camouflage the pond edge.

Photo by Oliver Jackson, courtesy of Custom Fountains

Careful selection and placement of stone hides the preformed pond edges.

Photo by Oliver Jackson

TIP

If the pond level appears uneven as the water is put in, grasp the pond edge and jiggle it until the level is restored.

Plants effectively conceal a preformed pond's edges.

Photo by H. Nash

TIP

A minimum of two inches of sand backfilled under and around the moulded pond will protect it from winter cracking and splitting.

entire form to this depth. Set the pond shell back on the site and mark around the pond's lowest level.

Once the excavation is completed, use a spirit level to verify the perfect levels of the shelf and bottom areas. Clear away any loose soil, rocks, or roots. Smooth a two-inch sand cushion over the entire bottom and shelves, tamping and carefully checking that the levels are maintained. Keep a hose handy, spraying the sand as necessary. Dry sand will easily slide off the shelf, fill in the bottom edge of the next level, and make level pond placement impossible.

Set the pond into its excavation and check the level of the top edges as the pond is filled with an inch or two of water. As the pond fills, gently backfill the sides with sand. Use a hose with the water running slowly to wash or flush the sand into the side excavation. Fill the pond nearly full, simultaneously washing sand down the sides of the excavation so that backfilling and waterfilling are performed at about the same level. Continue to monitor the level of the pond's top edge.

Once the pond has been backfilled to the excavated level for the edge reinforcement and the top edge is perfectly level, the edging reinforcement can be installed. This may be a concrete collar, concrete-reinforced soil, or a layer of crushed stone, as necessary. (See Chapter 9 for edging completion.)

If a waterfall or water course is planned in conjunction with the pond, see Chapter 8 for procedure.

Chapter Four
LINED POND CONSTRUCTION

Lined ponds can be very small.

Photo by T.J. Smith

TIP

Walk barefoot on liners so you can feel any rocks beneath that might puncture it.

If any one product can be credited with revolutionizing water gardening, it would have to be the flexible liner. Although some enthusiastic would-be-water-gardeners have used the least expensive and most readily-available materials, such as thin plastics or swimming pool liners, these liners are not suitable for water garden ponds. Even heavier grades of plastic sheeting puncture easily and degrade quickly, often in less than three years. Vinyl swimming pool liners may be treated with algicides that prove toxic over time to fish and plants. Also, their light color appears artificial.

In the past, PVC liners were commonly used for water gardens. More durable than plastic sheeting, they could be expected to last 10 to 15 years. However, they needed special care to protect them from the degrading UV sunlight.

While butyl was the liner of choice, offering elasticity, durability, and stability, it was expensive. However, Firestone Rubber Company in the United States developed a comparable synthetic rubber sheeting, EPDM, ethylene propylene diene monmer, commonly called PondGard™. This black, flexible liner with a 50-year life expectancy offers the same positive qualities of the butyl and is priced competitively.

Lined ponds can also be very large.

Photo by Eamonn Hughes

UNDERLAYS

Always use some form of protection or underlay between a flexible liner and the pond excavation. Some sources suggest old pieces of carpet. Joe B. Dekker of Aquascapes in Wycliff, New Jersey, has advocated the use of layers of newspaper to an inch thickness. Joe has noted that years later, in re-excavating a pond, the newspaper underlay had deteriorated into a powdery form called "gley." Joe notes the example of a fluid poured into dry flour—the liquid is repelled. The application of this principle in flexible liner construction means that small puncture holes in the liner do not result in water losses as the water is repelled by the powder-degraded form of newspaper on the excavation side of the liner.

Special synthetic fabric underlays or geo-thermal textiles are also available. These products are strong enough to protect the liner from potential punctures caused by sharp rocks working their way up through the soil. A new development is EPDM sheeting with the underlay bonded to it.

Whatever choice of underlay is chosen, some form is advisable. Where large rocks or concrete blocks are placed on top of the liner, it may be wise to supply a layer of the protective fabric on top of the liner, too.

CALCULATING LINER SIZE

Although the liner size may be calculated and purchased before the excavation, it is a good idea to wait until the excavation is completed and final measurements can be taken. Unless any sidewalls, including shelves, are only gently sloped, the shelves

> ### TIP
> Indoor-outdoor carpet used as underlay should be slashed, to prevent collected water from lifting the liner.

should be added into the computation. The base figures come from the maximum width and length of the pond, regardless of shape. Add to each figure any depths from top to shelf, from shelf to bottom, or top to bottom, as the case may be. If the entire pond has a planting shelf, the depths of the top to the shelf and the shelf to the pond bottom may be doubled to account for the same measurements on the opposite side. *The depth figures must account for the depths on opposite sides of the pond and must be added to both the width and length base figures.* At least an extra foot should be added to the width and length figures to allow for an extra six inches around the upper edge that will come up behind the pond edging.

Liner Size: Maximum Length + 2 Depths + 1 Foot × Maximum Width + 2 Depths + 1 Foot

BASIC INSTALLATION OF A FLEXIBLE LINER

As with any other type of water garden installation, the levels should be estab-lished *before* any excavation is begun. With a lined pond, the shelves and pond bottom need not be perfectly level; it is the *upper* edge of the pond that determines that the water level will be the same on all sides of the pond.

Soil-type permitting, the sides of the pond should be excavated as steeply as pos-sible. This allows the top edging to best conceal the liner. Vertical sides coming down from plant shelves will make it easy to step out of the pond; a sloped side will be slippery and dangerous to walk on when it is necessary to be in the pond. Naturally, clay soils are the easiest to carve shelves and pond sides into. Should the soil be sandy or loamy, make the slope more grad-ual. This is appropriate only for a very shallow or a very large water garden. Wooden forms, concrete collars, concrete blocks, or LineUps™ may be necessary to form the pond sides. (See Chapter 2)

Although many commercial sources show installation directly into the soil, such installations are not as durable in the long run as installations that include suita-ble side reinforcements to support heavy stonework and planting shelves. Pond sides may deteriorate beneath the liner, the sides may bulge outward from water pressure and pull the liner down, perhaps creating water losses, and stonework may settle and dis-rupt the level of the pond. Even though the sides are excavated nearly vertically, only the heaviest of clay soils can be expected to hold its shape properly.

Likewise, make provisions at the top edge of the pond to accommodate the weight of any stone used. A clean, sharp edge is mandatory as stone will rest upon the level area. Particularly if crushed stone is to be used to provide support for stone-work, some manner of edge formwork will

Flexible EPDM PondGard™ liners are easy to move into the excavation.

Photo courtesy of Firestone Building Products

SOLUTION SIMPLE LINER CONSTRUCTION

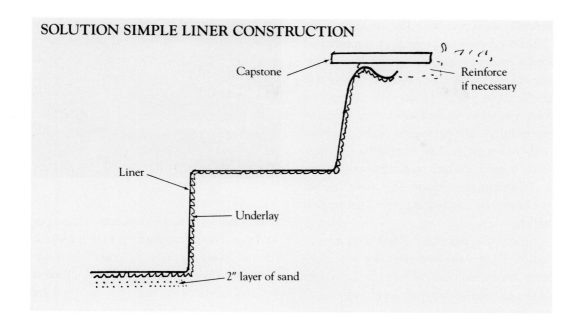

be necessary. Crushed stone, like sand, will not hold a firm edge. (See Chapter 2 for side and edge reinforcement constructions.)

The process of excavation proceeds with sod removal, pond-outline marking on the ground, and soil removal one shovelful deep at a time. Once the hole is deep enough to accommodate the planting shelf, mark the outer edge of the shelf so it will be 18 to 36 inches wide. Then dig out the next level of the pond. The final depth should be sloped slightly to one place to facilitate pond drainage. The shelf and the pond bottom need not be perfectly level; they need be only level enough that plant pots can be set upon them. The upper pond edge, however, *must be perfectly level*.

Clear the excavation of loose soil and any protruding roots or loose stones. Smooth a two-inch layer of sand over the bottom. Spread sand on the shelf surface, but keep it suitably moist to prevent it from sliding down and creating a slope to the wall. Carefully fit an underlay over the entire excavation. If the underlay is cut from several pieces, it may be necessary to anchor it in places with bricks or stone.

As the sand and underlay are installed, the pond liner may be unfolded to warm in the sun. This will help to ease any creases and fold marks. Butyl and EPDM Pond-Gard™ will not have fold marks. If the day is sunny and hot, black liners will be quite hot to touch. Thin garden gloves may be necessary to protect hands from burns.

Drape the liner gently in the excavation so that at least six inches is in excess fully around the perimeter. If the pond is so large that setting the open liner into the excavation is cumbersome, fold it in half and lay it into the hole, unfolding it gently. Remove any weights on the underlay in the process.

Although some pond installation directions suggest anchoring the liner loosely in the hole and allowing the filling water to pull it down, this may not be the wisest way to proceed. EPDM or butyl liners are not likely to develop weak spots from being stretched, but other liner materials may be seriously weakened and develop holes later.

Most professional installers smooth and fit the liner into the excavation *before* adding any water. Whatever the shape of the pond, a flat piece of liner will need to be folded in spots to conform to the shape of the pond. While fitting the liner, combine folds to create as few as possible. Corner folds mitred inwards will appear smooth and flat from the outside. The more flexible the liner, the easier and better looking this will be.

Once the liner is folded and fitted, lightly anchor the excess at the top edges with stones or bricks. When the top edges of the excavation are fully level, begin adding the water. Monitor the folds and adjust them as necessary while the water level rises. Fill the pond as near to the top as desired to ascertain the level of the top edge and the settled fitting of the liner. The pond can be left alone for a day or two to allow for any liner settling. When it is time to finish the top edging, use the submerged recycling pump to remove enough water to work comfortably around the edge. (See Chapter 9 for edging completion.)

FLEXIBLE LINER INSTALLED BEHIND POND WALLS

Installing the liner *behind* the walls of the

pond lends itself to formal constructions, as well as to beautiful adaptations of informal, natural looking ponds. A formal construction might use bricks as the interior pond wall, or perhaps concrete blocks that are then sealed with black waterproof sealant or neoprene paint. Informal ponds would have walls of stone, cobbles, or layered rubble.

The critical factor in mortared construction within the pond is to neutralize any mortar or concrete properly. This is likely to involve several water changes once the pond has been completed. Using vinegar in the first water change can speed up the process. Waterproof paint or sealant is another option.

Naturally, constructing walls of brick or stonework means that the walls will be totally vertical. Such weight needs adequate support to prevent it from settling into the ground. The best way to support such walls is to install a concrete footing all the way around the pond base. This footing can be extended as a concrete base for the pond bottom, too. (See Chapter 5)

Problems can later arise if the concrete footings are installed above the frost line. In central Indiana, for example, it is recommended that any concrete footings be three feet deep. Areas colder than Zone 5 require even deeper footings. Obviously, this is deeper than the usual two feet planned for a water garden. Considering the time, expense, and expertise required to pour such thick layers of concrete, a layer of compacted, crushed stone and sand might be a practical choice.

Excavate the pond to the desired depth, and follow the procedure for concrete collar/footing construction described in Chapter Two, working to the appropriate frost-line depth. Once the concrete footing has cured, concrete block construction can be used up to the pond bottom. Either construct a concrete base beneath or on top of the liner or follow the compacted-soil-with-sand-covering for the pond bottom.

Next, lay the liner into the excavation, folding as necessary. Anchor the edges of the liner securely around the top perimeter. Cut a double piece of underlay and place it around the bottom edge over the footing of concrete blocks or cement. Spread newspapers or a tarp of some sort on the pond bottom to facilitate cleaning. Build the pond walls as described in Chapter Five, making certain that the work proceeds upward perfectly level and that no sharp edges protrude from the back that might puncture the liner. (Smooth any squeezed mortar flush with the back of the wall.) The wall should be constructed towards the back of the concrete footing for the greatest stability.

Once the walls are to the edging level, gently pull the liner up and weight it on top in order to backfill behind the wall. Professional backfill material is a lean mortar or lean concrete mix. This may be mixed heavily with soil backfill. Dry "cement soil," discussed in Chapter Two, may also be firmly tamped into the excavation. (See edging completion in Chapter 9.)

FLEXIBLE LINER CONSTRUCTED WITHIN WALLS

This construction method is similar to that of a wall built inside the liner. Excavate wide enough to accommodate double-wall construction and deep enough for a footing below the frost line.

Once the concrete footing has cured and will support the wall, construct a concrete-block wall. Maintain a perfect level up to the ground's surface. Build the wall on the back half of the footing.

Tamp the base of the pond well and cover it with sand. Place a protective underlay inside the excavation and fit the liner, folding as necessary. The fitting may be aided by spacing bricks around the inside bottom perimeter, around the back of any shelves, and around the top edge. Next, fit a second layer of underlay over the liner where the inner wall will sit upon the liner. Construct the inner wall with the stonework supported by the inner half of the concrete footing.

Before constructing the capping, backfill between the ground and the outer wall construction. This backfilling can be lean concrete (8:1 aggregate to cement), stiff concrete mixed in with the backfill soil, or ample dry concrete mixed in the backfill soil. (See Chapter 9 for edging constructions.)

TIP
Any footing constructed for pond walls must be perfectly level.

TIP
Save some money by constructing the lowest portion of the inner pond wall with concrete blocks; then paint them with a camouflaging black sealant.

Chapter Five

CONCRETE CONSTRUCTIONS

Although the development of strong, flexible EPDM-type liners have virtually replaced the idea that a long-lived pond must be constructed of concrete, concrete may still be the construction method of choice. Successful concrete ponds, particularly large ones, are best constructed by professionals. The do-it-yourselfer should start out with a small concrete project, such as a fountain basin or a small water feature.

A simple concrete construction finished in black marble creates an elegant water feature.

Photo by Lee Dreyfuss

A semi-raised construction is appropriate for a concrete atrium pond.

Photo by Bill Marocco, courtesy of Wabash National Corporation

TIP

When mixing stone aggregate into a concrete mix, the stone must be clean; dirt will prevent a good bond and weaken the concrete. Likewise, water added to the mix must be very clean.

THE BASICS OF CONCRETE

Concrete is made of specific amounts of cement, sand, gravel, and water. Mortar is similar but has no gravel in the mix. Both may be purchased premixed in 80-pound bags. Each makes up ⅔ cubic foot. Water is the catalyst that causes the material to harden; the less water, the stronger the mix and the stiffer it is to work.

A good mix, well-tamped, is primary. Weather is a critical factor: freezing conditions invite disintegration of the concrete before it has cured, and very hot conditions may allow it to dry too quickly, likewise resulting in a weak, disintegrating product. Use acid-resistant cement in very acidic soil to prevent disintegration.

Concrete work should use reinforcing mesh, or in larger or steep-sided areas, reinforcing rods and expansion joints. Bury such reinforcements inside the concrete at least one inch from the outer surface. Any overlapping reinforcements should be tied together with wire.

Concrete for the entire project should be

TIP

Use a garden hoe to mix concrete and mortar in a wheelbarrow. A common mistake is adding too much water; add more cement mix to achieve a proper stiffness.

TIP

Installing a bottom drain may be more trouble than it's worth. So long as the pond bottom slopes to a deeper level or to a sump area, the submerged pump may be used to empty the pond.

TIP

Install any pipes or electrical wiring prior to the concrete pour.

poured the same day to prevent weak joints that will crack with temperature changes. Cracks are difficult to repair with any assurance they won't reoccur at the same place. Verify that any sealant/paint over-coating bonds well to concrete.

To prevent harm to fish, smooth the inner walls with a coat of rendering. Neutralize any concrete or mortar used around the pond or treat it with a sealant to prevent lime from leaching into the water and jeopardizing the fish.

Even the most expertly built concrete pond is offered long-term protection if it is constructed within and upon a sturdy EPDM-type membrane. Establishing levels before starting and frequently verifying during the construction process is essential if the final product is to be perfectly level. Excavation should accommodate the following base and wall thicknesses:

4 to 6 inches for small ponds
6 to 8 inches for medium-sized ponds
8 to 10 inches for large ponds

Suggested Concrete Mixes

Foundations and footings:	1 part cement to 2 parts sharp sand to 4 parts aggregate
Pond bases and walls:	1 part cement to 2 parts sharp sand to 3 parts ¼–1-inch aggregate
Waterproof rendering:	1 part cement to 3 parts builders' sand plus waterproofing agent

Additives

Here are some substances that can supplement a regular mix and the reasons for their use:

Air-entraining agent—millions of tiny air bubbles are trapped in the concrete to prevent the concrete from cracking in cold climates. A concrete mixer is required.
Calcium chloride—this makes concrete set more rapidly than usual, thereby preventing freezing and expansion, which can fracture the pour.
Set-retarding agent—used in weather hotter than 90°F, to keep the concrete from setting too fast.
Plasticizer—this additive reduces the amount of water in the mix, preventing excessive shrinking and cracking.
Color agents—these should be added during the mixing process to color the concrete.

PREPARING THE SITE

Check and stake levels! Once installed, the level of a concrete pond cannot be altered without inviting weakened areas, recurring repairs, and frustration.

Be sure the excavation will allow for appropriate base and wall thicknesses. Spread a good layer of compacted hardcore into the pond base. The base and sides should be firmly tamped before constructing the concrete forms.

Be sure all supplies are on hand as you begin work. You don't want to near the end of construction and discover you haven't enough reinforcing material or cement!

CONSTRUCTING THE CONCRETE POND

It is assumed the excavation allows for perfectly level top edges and base and wall thicknesses, as well as that the excavation has been smoothed, the soil tamped firmly, and well-tamped hardcore reinforcement covers the base. Because a durable liner is

CONCRETE BASE CONSTRUCTION

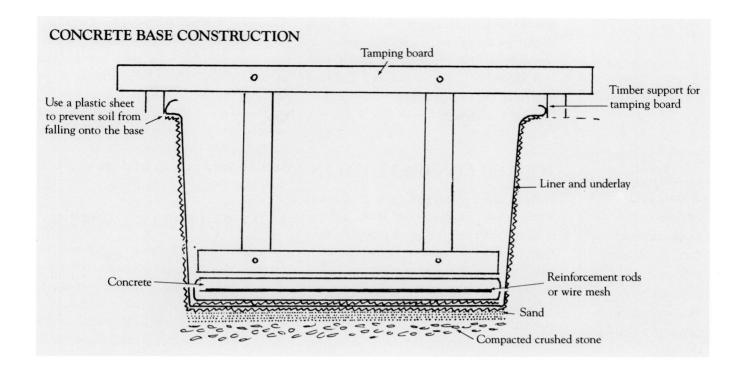

Tamping board

Use a plastic sheet to prevent soil from falling onto the base

Timber support for tamping board

Liner and underlay

Concrete

Reinforcement rods or wire mesh

Sand

Compacted crushed stone

recommended beneath the pond construction, a suitable underlay may also be provided.

Plan to begin the concreting at an early enough hour in the day to complete the work within one day—both base and walls must be poured on the same day. If trucks of concrete are to be brought in, try to coordinate delivery so that the work may proceed simultaneously. Be sure to have enough friends, relatives, and neighbors on hand to keep the process moving!

Concrete forms should be in place before the pour. If walls are to be constructed of concrete blocks, they may be constructed the day after the base is poured. However, the newly poured base will need to be protected with wooden planks.

Base Construction

Pour in concrete and tamp it down as you work backwards. Larger-size ponds will merit the use of a tamping board. (See above.) One complete layer of concrete 2 to 6 inches thick is poured and tamped.

Next, position wire mesh or metal rods over the fresh concrete. Apply a second layer of concrete of approximately the same thickness. (If the second layer cannot be poured in the same day, roughen the surface of the first layer with a stiff brush while it is still wet. The following day, lay the reinforcing materials and thoroughly wet the first layer of concrete before applying the second layer.) The thickness of the two layers will depend upon the climate zone: temperate climates will do fine with 4 to 6 inches in total, while northern climates may require as much as 12 to 15 inches in total thickness.

If a professional will come in and spray the concrete into the form, have both the base and the sides constructed in one application for a seamless pond form. Position

TIP

Clay soil shrinks during dry spells. A layer of crushed stone between the clay and the concrete helps to prevent cracking.

TIP

Any reinforcing metals that protrude from concrete may oxidize and create leaks in the concrete form.

the base reinforcements at the center level of the total thickness and then bring up the sides. The reinforcing mesh and rods should be fully constructed and tied carefully at any overlaps to allow the sprayed concrete to flow freely around them.

POURED CONCRETE WALLS

Vertical sides require the use of wooden forms known as shuttering. If the pond is informal with gently sloping slides, shuttering may not be required. However, even the informal pond that features heavy architectural structures weighing on the sides will require shuttering for maximum strength.

While the concrete base is still wet, roughen the edges with a stiff brush to provide maximum bonding potential with the walls. Any reinforcement that was used in the base should be upturned and extended into the bonding area of the walls. Prebent rods are available of 12 inches or more in length from the bend; these rods provide maximum strength at base-and-wall joinings.

Shuttering of the same thickness is installed and held in place with crosspieces. *Be sure the top of the shuttering is perfectly level!* The shuttering boards should not cut into any corners of the pond or they will create weak points in the structure. Vacuum out any debris that falls into your excavation during the work. Avoid this problem by lining the excavation with a plastic dropcloth. If a joint is formed between the pond base and the walls, keep it especially clean, hosing it if necessary.

As the side forms are filled with concrete, tamp the concrete down firmly with a wooden rammer. The top edge of the wall should be troweled perfectly level with the form on the pond's inner edge. Troweling with a slight slope back towards the surrounding ground facilitates edge construction.

Should the sides be uneven, fill the gaps with concrete by supplying additional shuttering. A gap left behind such an area can later be filled in with hardcore or a lean concrete mix.

CONCRETE BLOCK WALLS

Using concrete blocks to construct the walls greatly simplifies a concrete construction. By their nature, however, concrete blocks are suited only to more formal, geometric designs. Solid, four-inch thick blocks are commonly used in pond construction, although larger, hollow blocks may be used as well. Hollow blocks must be filled with a strong mix of concrete as they are laid. Even greater strength is achieved with a double wall of hollow blocks and the area between them filled with concrete.

An advantage to block walls is that they may be installed the day after the concrete base is poured. Be sure to roughen the base edges where the blocks will join while the concrete is still wet. Reinforcing rods should extend out and up into the area where the blocks will sit to create a solid joint. The reinforcing rods should extend up the back or ground-side of the wall construction in solid concrete-block walls. Naturally, it is imperative that the perimeter base of the pond be perfectly level since concrete blocks are preformed. Extra care, as well, should be taken to maintain consistency in the thickness of the mortar between the wall blocks. (See Chapter 2 for mortaring of blocks.) When building up the block walls, remember to plan for a thick layer of mortar to embed the pond edging in. If necessary, replace the top layer of blocks with solid, engineering bricks to accommodate the height requirements.

To accommodate shelf construction, the bottom wall of the pond may be two or three blocks wide and then drop back to a narrower width. Wider shelves can be constructed similarly, shaping the excavation to fit such constructions. A concrete footing is generally advised for support of the shelf walls if a concrete base is not provided.

Concrete and massive stone combine to make a spectacular water feature.

Photo by Deb Moak

CONCRETE BLOCK CORNER CONSTRUCTION

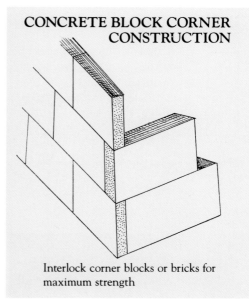

Interlock corner blocks or bricks for maximum strength

TIP

A pH reading over 8.5 indicates the presence of lime from concrete or mortar in the pond water. The source of the lime should be removed or treated before fish are introduced into the pond.

CONCRETE BLOCK WALL CONSTRUCTION

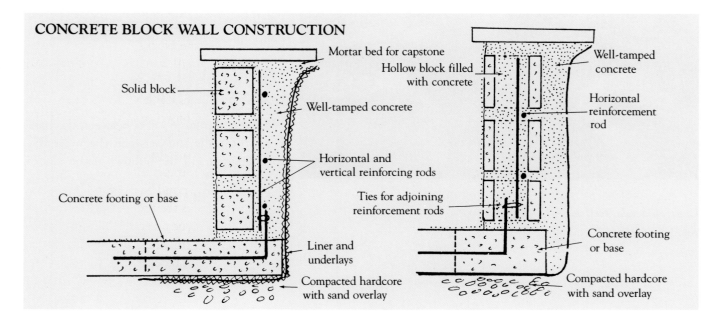

Solid block

Concrete footing or base

Mortar bed for capstone

Hollow block filled with concrete

Well-tamped concrete

Horizontal and vertical reinforcing rods

Ties for adjoining reinforcement rods

Liner and underlays

Compacted hardcore with sand overlay

Well-tamped concrete

Horizontal reinforcement rod

Concrete footing or base

Compacted hardcore with sand overlay

CONCRETE BLOCK POND CONSTRUCTION

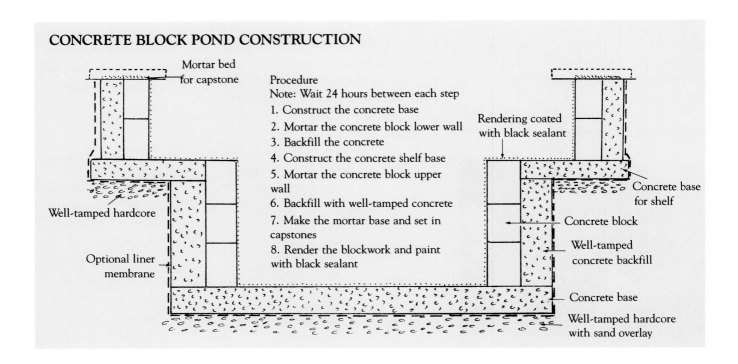

Mortar bed for capstone

Well-tamped hardcore

Optional liner membrane

Procedure

Note: Wait 24 hours between each step

1. Construct the concrete base
2. Mortar the concrete block lower wall
3. Backfill the concrete
4. Construct the concrete shelf base
5. Mortar the concrete block upper wall
6. Backfill with well-tamped concrete
7. Make the mortar base and set in capstones
8. Render the blockwork and paint with black sealant

Rendering coated with black sealant

Concrete base for shelf

Concrete block

Well-tamped concrete backfill

Concrete base

Well-tamped hardcore with sand overlay

Concrete lends itself to informal designs.

Photo by Cla Allgood

SOLID-BLOCK CONSTRUCTION

This type of construction requires that a good-sized cavity be left behind the wall construction for concrete backfilling. The wall-base joint should be reinforced with appropriate rods, as discussed above.

HOLLOW-BLOCK CONSTRUCTION

Properly reinforce joints between the base and the walls and between the walls and the edging. Fill the hollows of the blocks with a 3:2:1 concrete mix. Place rebar in the center of the hollows every 2 or 3 blocks.

EXTRA REINFORCEMENT

Reinforcing rods or strong mesh can be used behind the solid block wall construction. Carefully tie the extended and upturned reinforcement from the pond base to such reinforcement behind the blocks. Firmly tamp down poured concrete behind the block wall.

Insert reinforcing rods or wire mesh in the centers of the hollow blocks. Attach the rods firmly to the reinforcement that extends from the pond base. Fill the hollows with well-tamped concrete.

Double-wall block construction requires the use of reinforcing rods or mesh in the cavity between the two walls, as well.

If you construct plant shelves of poured concrete, be sure to reinforce them adequately.

RENDERING CONCRETE

Rendering is important to give a smooth finish to the final surface of the concreted pond. Especially during spawning, fish may brush against the pond walls and suffer injuries that can develop into bacterial infections. A smooth finish is also more comfortable to work around while tending the water garden.

A rendering coat should be three parts sand to one part portland cement. It can be applied within a day or two of the concrete's hardening. Waterproofing involves using an additive in either liquid or powder form. A black pigment can also be added to the mix to give the pond a natural, deep appearance.

A similar option is black, neoprene paint. This product should be fish-safe and applied in two separate coats, with a good drying period between applications.

COMBINING CONCRETE AND FLEXIBLE LINERS

The method of using a concrete pond form either beneath or over a flexible EPDM liner combines the best of both worlds. The liner is not affected by temperature extremes, while the concrete provides necessary support for the pond and its edging. Because clay soils can shrink in dry periods and looser soils can shift and settle, the concrete form provides an often-needed stability.

If the liner is used over the concrete, it is not necessary for the concrete sub-pond to

Rebar reinforces hollow concrete blocks for strength and stability.
Photo by Oliver Jackson

Using a liner beneath concrete constructions ensures cracks do not become leaks.
Photo by H. Nash

be as thickly constructed. Even though the concrete beneath may crack from weather or ground shifts, the liner remains supported and intact.

Such support is also possible simply by mixing a stiff concrete mix into a couple of inches of the pond excavation and tamping it firmly.

Whether a thin concrete shell or a concrete-reinforced soil base is used, an underlay will protect the liner from pressure abrasions caused by the water or the weight of people or plants.

WORKING WITH MORTAR

Mortar is very similar to concrete except it does not contain stone aggregate and therefore lacks the strength of concrete. Mortar is used to embed stonework or bricks and create seals between them. It is *not* an all-purpose glue. Any stonework used with mortar should first fit where it is placed.

Masonry mortar has a bit more flexibility than regular mortar mixes; it contains lime, which helps the mix resist cracking from temperature changes. Although mortar comes premixed in 80-pound bags, in both the regular and the masonry mixes, it is less expensive to mix your own if large quantities are to be used. *A standard mortar mix is 1 part lime, 2 parts portland cement, and 9 parts sharp sand.*

Be sure it is thoroughly dry-mixed with a hoe or shovel before adding water. A large wheelbarrow is a convenient mixing container. Add water a bit at a time and mix with the hoe. The mortar should stand in peaks and create suction when a trowel is wiggled flat into it. If the mix is too thin, it will run; if it is too thick, it will not bond well.

Stop adding water just before you think it's enough—it seems to turn runny with the last cup added. If the mix is runny, add more premix or more cement and sand. Alternatively, let the mix rest for half an hour to allow the water to rise to the surface and then pour it off carefully. If the mixture is not too runny, wait until the water starts to rise to the surface and begin working with the stiffer mortar from the bottom of the mix.

In working with stone, spread a one-inch-thick layer of mortar and rock the stone firmly into place. This will push out some of the mortar, which is then trimmed with the trowel. In working with brick, the brick is "buttered" before placing it on a thin layer of mortar.

To get mortar into a joint from the outside after the stone or brick is in place, put a little mortar on the bottom edge of the trowel, near the tip, and smear it into the crevice with a push-and-wipe action. This is called "pointing up." Mortar should be uniformly recessed so the stonework appears to be jutting out from a recessed wall beneath it. Recessing can be performed up to 12 hours after the work has been done. After the mortar is crumbly, a wire brush can be used to finish the recessing.

Curing both mortar and cement allows the chemical action to be completed. The work must be kept moist for up to six days. Cover the area with plastic sheets or wet burlap. Once the mortar or concrete has set and won't wash or run out, moisten it with a hose twice a day, more frequently in hot weather.

Even the neatest mortaring will have smears and stains on the workface. Some can be removed during the crumbly stage of curing with a wire brush. Stubborn stains can be removed with a solution of 1 part muriatic acid to 10 parts water.

TIP

For the strongest mortared wall, lay only three vertical courses a day. Work carefully around the "green" layers from the day before.

Chapter Six

RAISED AND SEMI-RAISED POND CONSTRUCTION

Constructing a water garden with the side walls at least partially raised above ground level has several advantages. While the actual pond construction is not less work than an in-ground construction, the amount of excavation is significantly lessened. Maintenance of the water garden is easier and the pond is much easier to clean and empty as well. Children are less likely to fall into the pond. People with back problems or disabilities will have fuller enjoyment of the garden, and everyone can enjoy a closer look at the life within the pond.

Problems can arise with raised ponds. They are more susceptible to fluctuations in water temperatures, which may stress fish. Likewise, in cold climates it may be necessary to provide extra depth or insulation to prevent the pond from freezing solidly in the winter.

Because raised or semi-raised ponds require vertical sides for strength, it is usually best to construct them as formally designed gardens. However, using mortared fieldstone or rubble in a circular form can accommodate a semi-formal scheme.

BASIC PRINCIPLES OF ABOVE-GROUND CONSTRUCTION

Excavation is the same as for an in-ground pond. Levels should be checked and maintained at every stage of construction.

Concrete footings, adequate hardcore,

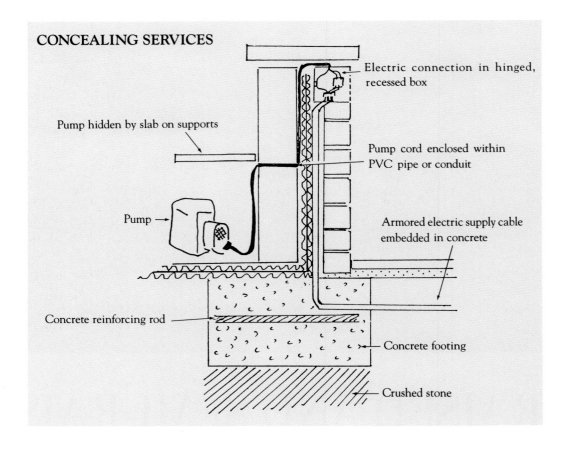

CONCEALING SERVICES

Electric connection in hinged, recessed box

Pump hidden by slab on supports

Pump cord enclosed within PVC pipe or conduit

Pump →

Armored electric supply cable embedded in concrete

Concrete reinforcing rod

Concrete footing

Crushed stone

or well-tamped, concrete-reinforced soil is necessary. Building the pond walls on soil alone invites collapse. Any pond built fully above ground should have a strong concrete foundation, to minimize potential damage from shifting soil and settling of the heavy, water-filled pond.

Since the water level is maintained up to the pond edging, mortar joinings of edging stones should be thin and inconspicuous. Flexible liners are fitted in the same manner as with in-ground construction and trimmed half-way over the top of the wall, to allow the edge of the wall to be mortared. Anywhere bricks may touch water, engineering-quality solid bricks will minimize frost/freezing damage. Neutralize concrete or mortar used in the pond itself or around the edging or treat it to prevent lime from leaching into the water. Before constructing the edge, leave a groove or space to accommodate electrical wiring if an electrical box is not built into the wall.

Outer walls should be at least nine inches thick to withstand water pressure, although a pond raised no more than 12 inches above ground may have but a single layer of bricks in the walls. Freezing climate zones should have well-reinforced, thicker walls or a double wall with insulation in the center.

Fiberglass preformed ponds are usually strong enough to require no additional wall support. Plastic preforms, however, will collapse without additional side support; simply piling soil around the walls is not enough.

The partially raised preform should be set in an excavation that allows the pond's shelf areas to sit level on the ground. A wall is then constructed to support the side walls above the ground.

BASIC CONSTRUCTION OF SEMI-RAISED POND WITH LINER

In excavation, allow for either single- or double-wall construction to the bottom of the pond. Solid or hollow nine-inch concrete blocks provide stable support. Render or plaster the outside of their visible upper section or cover them with bricks or stonework.

Install a footing twice the width of the wall and at least six inches thick into the pond bottom. If the frost line is too deep to make a concrete footing practical, dig the trench deep enough for a well-tamped base of several inches of crushed stone which the footing will be constructed on. Consult local building suppliers for recommended depths and thicknesses.

The in-ground wall may be constructed of concrete blocks and then more attractive decorative stonework used for the wall rising above ground.

Be sure the mortar used in the wall construction has sufficient time to cure and the walls are perfectly level before setting the liner. The bottom of the pond should be well tamped, padded with a few inches of sand, and then a protective underlay provided for the entire pond. Colder climates may require a layer of insulation, such as styrofoam sheets or wall/roof insulation under the liner or between double walls. Do not use insulation on the bottom of the pond.

Carefully fit the liner into the pond form and weight it around the top wall. Square-corner fitting requires weighting the smoothed bottom at the base of the walls. Smooth the liner flat against the walls and gather the excess loosely in the corners. Trim the membrane to overlap only to the outer wall edge. Use one hand to tuck the excess liner into a fold against the pond wall to create a straight-edged fold up the corner. Repeat this process on the adjoining wall section and in the remaining corners. Circular liner fittings proceed in the same manner, with folds created as needed. In each fold, the excess liner is folded in to the wall. Fill the pond with a couple of inches of water, to be certain the liner is well fitted and won't pull down into the excavation when the pond is full. Filling the pond completely verifies that the walls are perfectly level and the water level is the same all around the pond perimeter. *If the water level is not equal all around the pond perimeter, fix the outer walls to be level before applying the edging.*

SEMI-RAISED POND WITH LINER BETWEEN WALLS

This construction also requires excavation to accommodate the wall thickness to the pond bottom. Dig a wide trench around the pond base within the excavation to accommodate the full thickness of the walls. Pour reinforced concrete footing flush with the pond bottom. Once the footing has set, build the outer wall from the outside edge of the footing, but fully supported by the footing. Smooth any oozing mortar on the pond side of the walls.

Be sure the pond bottom is smooth and free of stones and rubble. Apply a two-inch layer of sand. Since both sides of the liner must be protected from potential punctures, prepare it for installation by sand-

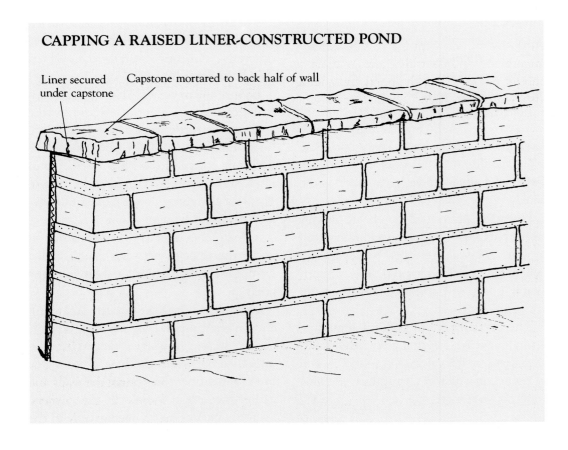

CAPPING A RAISED LINER-CONSTRUCTED POND

Liner secured under capstone   Capstone mortared to back half of wall

wiching it between two full-sized pieces of fabric underlay. This additional thickness makes the folds more cumbersome, but they will not be visible when the pond is completed. After fitting the liner into the excavation, anchor it securely around the bottom and top of the wall.

Construct the inner wall directly on the liner so it sits on the inner edge of the footing constructed beneath the liner. (A concrete base may also be constructed directly on the liner with the inner wall joined into it. The concrete pond base should be at least four inches thick, the application consisting of two inches of concrete, a layer of reinforcement, and the final two inches of concrete. The excavation, as well as the liner size, needs to be figured to accommodate these extra thicknesses.)

Verify the accuracy of the levels before finishing the top edging. Be sure to cure, waterproof, and neutralize any concrete or mortar before filling the pond and adding fish and plants. (See Chapter 9 for edging construction.)

SEMI-RAISED CONSTRUCTION WITH PREFORMED PONDS

This form of construction is easiest with a symmetrically shaped preformed shell. After checking the site levels, mark around the shell's outer dimensions. (See Chapter 3.) Be sure the excavation allows for two extra inches of sand cushioning. A perfectly level concrete footing or a base six to nine inches deep may also be constructed for the shell to sit upon, if necessary. The sand cushion would then be placed on the concrete. Be certain that the shell, when set in its excavation, is perfectly level at the top edge.

Construct a level concrete footing as a base for the outer wall per locally recommended specifications. (See Chapter 2 for concrete footing and wall constructions.) After the wall has cured, backfill between the wall and the pond form with sand. Add water to the shell during the backfilling to prevent the sand from lifting the shell and spoiling the established level.

The concrete footing is marked to guide in block placement.

Photo courtesy of Firestone Building Products

Mortar is kept nearby.

Photo courtesy of Firestone Building Products

Mortar is lined onto the concrete footing.

Photo courtesy of Firestone Building Products

1. The block is aligned with the marked guide and mortar lines.

2. A block is "buttered" where it will adhere to others.

3. Check levels as you work. Tap blocks into alignment as necessary.

4. Working from both ends of the wall, the overall level is checked.

5. Alignment is also checked along the outer wall.

6. Levels of the installed blocks are monitored.

7. Half blocks are used for the top layer to achieve the desired height.

8. Insulation is provided between the wall and backfilling.

Photos courtesy of Firestone Building Products

1

5

2

6

3

7

4

8

9

10

11

12

13

14

9. Engineering bricks are "buttered" and faced onto the wall; the alignment and levels are again checked.

Photo by Oliver Jackson

10. Mortar is pointed between the bricks and brushed away.

Photo courtesy of Firestone Building Products

11. The pond is ready for lining.

Photo by Oliver Jackson

12. Once the liner is set, its edge is trimmed so mortar can be placed on the back half of the wall.

Photo by Oliver Jackson

13. Capstones are placed and pressed onto the wall leaving ¼" between them.

Photo by Oliver Jackson

14. The sides and ends of the gap are duct-taped to ease cleanup. Mortar is filled into the gaps.

Photo by H. Nash

15. *The pond is completed with a surrounding sand layer base for maintenance-free paving.*

Photo by Oliver Jackson

A raised pond completes the stepped waterfall set into a hillside.

Photo by Greg Speichert.
Courtesy of Gilburg Perennials

Chapter Seven

EARTH POND CONSTRUCTION

A water courseway and falls add an extra dimension to an earth pond.

Photo by Greg Maxwell

In Bay View, Michigan, a spring-fed drainage ditch was converted into a small, natural pond suitable for water lilies and surrounding bog plants.

Photo by H. Nash

Earth pond construction is not suitable generally for water gardens, which are small relative to the half-acre or more "farm ponds." Because resources are limited on these constructions, this chapter serves primarily to direct further research.

Probably the most important consideration is who you hire to do the excavation. It is not enough simply to find somebody with a bulldozer, backhoe, or other large digging equipment. Just as with the smaller water garden, levels are extremely important. The excavator must be adept in both the use of level equipment and the artful creation of a pond shell. Strange as it may sound, some excavators will simply pile up the spoil around the edges and count that height as part of the pond depth. And some excavators will check the levels of the pond *bottom* rather than the top edges! It is wise to check references and to see completed projects before committing to hire an excavator.

Other considerations in selecting an excavator are his knowledge and concept of drainage and the existing watersheds. Chances are you will have to arrange to haul away dirt, too. Be sure to have an on-site place to store your topsoil. Check around for the current prices of non-pulverized topsoil by the truckload and then offer it to your excavator, if you have no use for the topsoil, in exchange for a reasonable reduction in his price.

Monitor the progress of the excavation. This will ensure that the excavation is performed properly and will account for your valuable topsoil and the excavator's actual working hours.

Before hiring an excavator, research the type of earth pond you wish to have. Wildlife plant nurseries, such as Kester's, in Wisconsin, offer invaluable information in their catalogs. Fish hatcheries, such as Zetts, in Pennsylvania, likewise offer good information regarding stocking levels, combinations, and maintenance of various game species of fish. State Departments of Natural Resources, agricultural extensions, and universities will also have pertinent information.

THE CLAY-LINED POND

Because clay is not one hundred percent watertight, pond construction must be large enough to allow for probable water loss. Water loss can occur from aquatic plants growing in the pond, tree roots that grow to the water source and form fibrous root masses, tunneling animals, and underground springs that fluctuate in flow. Water loss can also occur if field drainage tiles are broken during construction. This allows water to enter from one end of the broken tile and leave by the other. (Plugging up such breakages can cause flooding problems "upstream.")

Clay that is encountered on-site should be very pure for water retention purposes. Blue clay usually indicates the presence of liquid, running sand, or water itself nearby.

It is important never to let the clay dry out during construction; apply soil or gravel over the clay to prevent drying. If the clay is dry, use a rototiller to powder up a five- or six-inch layer that will act as a sealant when the pond is filled.

This spring-fed, shallow pond will be the home of many water lilies and much wildlife.

Photo by Oliver Jackson

Water is recycled from an earth pond through an adjacent lined pond.

Photo by T.J. Smith

A standpipe connected to a drainage tile beneath the newly dug pond will accommodate rain overflows.

Photo by Oliver Jackson

Begin excavation at the deepest point with a method called "clay puddling," which is used to attain more water-retention capacity. This method involves compacting the wet clay as it is worked, either with feet, rammers, or mechanical compactors. The excavation is then filled partially as work proceeds outward from the center.

THE BENTONITE POND

Bentonite is a form of clay that is formed by fossilized volcanic ash. It is named for Fort Benton, Montana, where it was first discovered. Sold in powdered form, it expands when moistened, to provide a waterproof seal.

Problems with its use involve high or fluctuating water tables, the presence of chalk or gravel, invasive tree roots and shore-side vegetation, as well as the pres-ence of ducks and geese. Obviously, conditions must be ideal if bentonite is to be used successfully. Hence, the subsoil of the site must be tested before a decision is made. If the subsoil contains chalk or limestone, calcium ions will replace the bentonite's sodium ions and seriously impair the expansive and sealing capacity of the bentonite.

If bentonite is the method of choice, the soil must first be prepared. The excavation depth should allow an additional foot for a layer of soil that will cover the bentonite. The base of the pond, as well as the sides, should be clean and smooth, fairly dry, and free of organic material. Excavate the sides to a gentle slope since the bentonite will not remain stationary on a steep slope.

Spread bentonite evenly over the entire pond surface at a density of 20 pounds per square yard. A rototiller may be used to work it into the subsoil to a four-inch depth. Then use a compactor over the entire surfacing. Spread one foot or more of subsoil or topsoil before filling the pond. As the moisture penetrates to the bentonite layer, the swelling and sealing occurs beneath the soil cover.

ESS-13 Sealant

ESS-13 is a non-petroleum, oil-based, resinous polymer emulsion that alters the physical shape, moisture content, particle charge, and surface tension of earth ponds to alleviate seepage loss of water. It can be applied in the soil-compaction stage of pond construction, as well as by a waterborne application through standing water to reduce seepage loss by 60 to 90 percent.

As a vegetable-oil-based product, ESS-13 can have a few temporary side ef-

The natural pond at Duncan Water Gardens is home to many fish and exotic fowl.

Photo by Bob Johnson

fects when applied through standing water. Depending on the application rate, the oil can coat the gills of fish and cause them to suffocate. The manufacturers recommend removing any valuable fish before introducing the treatment.

Since it is a white oil, it will turn the water white for anywhere from a few days to several weeks. Likewise, it will cling to submerged aquatic plants and cause them to take on a whitish tinge. Neither side effect is permanent.

The product can also collect dust that appears as a whitish scum around the pond shore. This is easily removed with a swimming pool skimmer.

Although ESS-13 will not stop running-water leaks, it is an effective method of seepage control. Applied in the compaction stage of construction of an earth pond that has no viable source of fresh water, it can mean the difference between a dry hole in the ground and a long-lived pond or lake.

ESS-13 is used to stem seepage problems in earth ponds.

Photo courtesy of Seepage Control

Chapter Eight

WATERFALL AND STREAM CONSTRUCTIONS

Moss-covered rocks add life and character to this Eamonn Hughes construction.

Photo by E. Hughes

TIP

The wider the waterfall spillway, the less the force of the water flow.

One factor that determines the type of moving water feature to include is water lilies. Since lilies are not happy with moving or splashing water, any feature that might disturb them must be at a distance and of such minimal effect to allow the lilies to bloom freely. While moving water is enjoyable to watch, its primary attraction is its *sound*. Both lilies and the sound of moving water can coexist if the sound is created in an upper basin with the actual entry into the pond at a minimal flow. This can be achieved by a two-tiered waterfall with the upper level providing the sound and the lower level providing a wide-lipped basin, good for a biological filter area of plants such as watercress, that dissipates the force of the entry-water into the pond.

Waterfalls present a constant source of water loss. They may be constructed of heavy stones that, although perfectly set initially, shift in time with ground settling and weather changes. Even moulded plastic or fiberglass watercourse sections have the potential to overflow or to develop leaks. What works today may not work next summer when plants have grown, fuzzy green stuff clings to rocks, or silt has collected in

Large rocks are carved into shallow basins to direct a gentle waterfall.

Photo by H. Nash

Breaking a longer drop into shorter sections produces the desired water movement.

Photo by Eamonn Hughes

Water tumbling down the face of cobblestones is another type of waterfall.

Photo by Lee Dreyfuss

nooks and crannies. Always line a water course properly.

While it is possible to cut the pond liner to extend into the waterfall or courseway, most waterfalls will be lined with a separate piece of membrane. This piece of liner should generously overlap the pond liner.

A sand cushion and underlay beneath the liner, as well as extra padding between the liner and any rocks sitting on it, are advisable. Be watchful for capillary action that draws the water up from the pond through fabric underlays. The underlay should be cut so that it provides a cushion for heavy rocks while still not touching even the highest water level in the pond. Folds in the liner can also contribute to capillary losses.

Waterfalls are usually constructed into a pile of soil from the pond excavation. To avoid an alien-looking construction, gently slope the waterfall spoil around the pond. The height of the waterfall should be in proportion to both the pond and the surrounding site.

Large, heavy stones need ample support. This may be nothing more than crushed stone or stiff concrete in the soil beneath

them, or it may be thick pads of concrete. Generally, rocks heavier than 100 pounds should have at least a four-inch thick concrete pad beneath them. Heavier rocks require the concrete base be properly reinforced with rebar.

LINED WATERFALL CONSTRUCTION

Once the waterfall shell has been dug out, lay in the liner and run some water through it to check levels and possible leakage points. Even though the levels may be fine at this point, monitor them throughout the construction.

Start at the bottom or entry-level into the pond. Rocks over which the water falls should be flat with a smooth, crisp edge at the front. If they don't have a crisp edge, the water may not fall cleanly over them, but rather dribble into the water. (A dribble at this point may be fine if the sound is to occur farther up the falls and a gentle entry into the pond is desired for the lilies' sake.)

Proceeding up the waterfall, keep the hose handy for testing the flow over the rocks. If a basin is constructed at this point, line its perimeters with natural-looking rocks and line the basin with pea gravel or cobbles.

The flat rocks the water flows over into the next level should be tilted slightly forward to ensure the water flow. Especially where flat rocks are stacked upon each other to create the falls, it is easy to "lose"

Waterfalls used with a pond create both sound and beauty.

Photo by Joe B. Dekker

water out the back and sides of the construction. Check the flow frequently with the hose. A small carpenter's level verifies the level of the front edge of the rocks.

Work to the top of the falls, checking levels of flat rocks and lining the course with rocks to conceal the liner that is drawn up the side to prevent water loss. Draw the liner up the sides even higher than is initially envisioned since plants and accumulated silt and debris may eventually raise the level of the water flow. Besides

---

TIP

Keep the waterfall tiers close together. Too great a drop results in the water drawing back to the face of the construction to produce a "wet wall."

TIP

Jeannette Streeter of The Stone Center suggests carving a groove an inch in on the underside of a flat spillway rock. If the water tries to run back under the rock, it will drop down upon encountering the "uphill" groove.

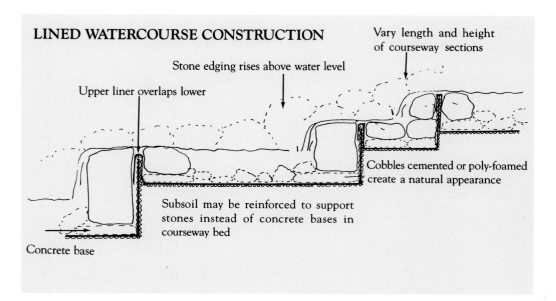

LINED WATERCOURSE CONSTRUCTION

Vary length and height of courseway sections

Stone edging rises above water level

Upper liner overlaps lower

Cobbles cemented or poly-foamed create a natural appearance

Subsoil may be reinforced to support stones instead of concrete bases in courseway bed

Concrete base

Native American–style waterfall captures Southwestern flavor.

Photo by Nancy Griego

TIP

Affix cobbles used in the water courseway to the liner with mortar, concrete, or poly foam to prevent the water from running under them instead of over them.

TIP

If a rock does not fit into the channel, dig more space out behind the liner to accommodate it.

A cobbled course directs rain runoff from a lined pond to the natural pond nearby.

Photo by T.J. Smith

water loss, nearby plants can die from too much water.

Pockets of soil behind rock edges and in nooks and crannies of the construction will support moisture-loving plants. Be certain the plants selected do not object to moving water. Bear in mind the ultimate size of plants chosen for these places. Heart-shaped bittercress, for example, may be only a few inches tall when planted, but will attain a height of two feet by mid-summer.

Stones at the side of the construction can be used to help direct the water flow over the falls. A stone placed into the water flow channel will change the direction and increase the force of the flow. If the rocks are being permanently affixed in the channel, experiment with the hose before making final placements.

Any significant water drops where the water will splash should have amply high walls to prevent water loss by redirecting the water back into the flow to the pond.

The top of the waterfall should be constructed to prevent the hose's visibility. Depending on personal preference, the initial water flow from the hose can be controlled. Water will appear to gush from its source if nothing is done to alter it. In the case of a very large waterfall, this may be desired. However, a smaller waterfall may look unnatural with so strong a flow.

Even though the mortar can be neutarlized, the water's pH level should be monitored to be sure it does not exceed 8.5. A second problem is relevant only to freezing climates. Mortar and concrete *will* crack and crumble resulting in yearly repairs.

Control the flow from the hosing by affixing a bar-tube to the end of the hose. This tube can have several holes bored along its length, with the end of the tube fully plugged. Water exiting from these several holes will be less vigorous.

Bill Dowden of Coastal Pond Supply has recommended that a watertight cavity be constructed at the top of the waterfall. He suggests that the outlet hose be directed *backwards* within this cavity so that the water flows up against the back wall of the cavity and then gently flows outward and over the construction. Likewise, a perforated bar-outlet can be directed away from the pond to allow for a more gentle flow.

It is tempting in constructing a waterfall to mortar everything in place. This can present two major problems. First of all, it creates a constant source of lime in the pond water that may be dangerous to fish.

An interesting alternative to concrete or mortar is quick-drying, poly foam, available from most building supply centers. The foam comes in a can and may be sprayed into any gaps between or behind rocks or around the edges of the construction, as well as between rocks and the liner. The foam actually bonds to the liner better than mortar. Joe B. Dekker recommends keeping a bucket of sand handy during the spraying operation. Wear gloves during the application and keep a stick handy to push

TIP
Water needs to gain speed to fall clear of a spillway. Providing a slight distance before the spillway helps prevent a wet wall.

the foam back into crevices and gaps. Quickly toss a handful of sand onto the surface, to camouflage its white or golden-yellow color. Check previously sprayed areas after a few minutes as bubbles of the foam may ooze through the sand. Once they have dried, these bubbles can be twisted or cut off with a razor blade. If the bare white of the foam is obtrusive, a dab of non-toxic paint can finish the camouflaging.

FORMAL WATERFALLS

Formal waterfalls are excavated like a staircase and constructed as detailed above, except that the materials used are of an appropriate nature—bricks, concrete, slabs, flagstone, or smooth paving slabs—to achieve the strict geometric structure of formal designs.

PREFORMED WATERFALL UNITS

Although limiting creative endeavors, preformed waterfall units are readily available in several variations that may be combined into a water course feature. They are available in plastic, fiberglass, cement, and reconstituted stone.

Excavate the area as necessary, compact the soil, and line it with a good layer of sand, placing a piece of liner over it. Set in the courseway section, backfilling beneath it with sand as needed, and pull the liner up

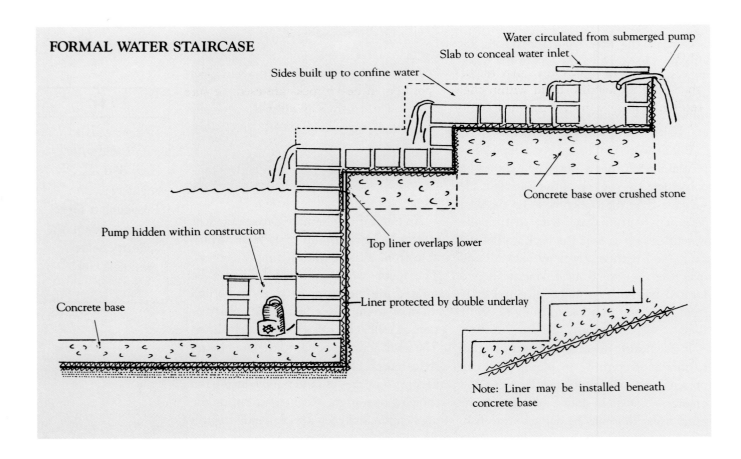

FORMAL WATER STAIRCASE

Water circulated from submerged pump

Slab to conceal water inlet

Sides built up to confine water

Concrete base over crushed stone

Pump hidden within construction

Top liner overlaps lower

Concrete base

Liner protected by double underlay

Note: Liner may be installed beneath concrete base

around the edges. Conceal the liner and moulded shell with soil and rocks.

Plastic and fiberglass units may require anchoring to stabilize them within their setting. This may involve the intrusion of rock formations around them, which will aid in making them look more natural. It is difficult to fully camouflage such features, even though manufacturers assure us that in time, mosses and such naturalize the feature. It can be a real challenge to cover them with enough rock to look natural while not disrupting the already perfected flowing levels.

Cement and reconstituted stone constructions may look a bit more natural. Set them in water to check the water's pH for leached lime. Coat them with a lime-neutralizer if necessary.

Several units can be combined to create a lengthier water course. Each unit must overlap the lower and be set firmly in a level position. If heavy rocks are used, be sure the soil beneath is reinforced to prevent settling in time. Be sure the water flowing through the course has at least an inch above it to contain it; some molded units do not have enough depth to accommodate rock linings or plants within them.

Preformed waterfall units are suitable for smaller water features. Installation of a single unit is fairly simple. Make sure the unit sufficiently overlaps the pond to direct the water. Arrange the desired camouflage around the unit to naturalize it in its setting. (Have an extra piece of liner beneath and around it.)

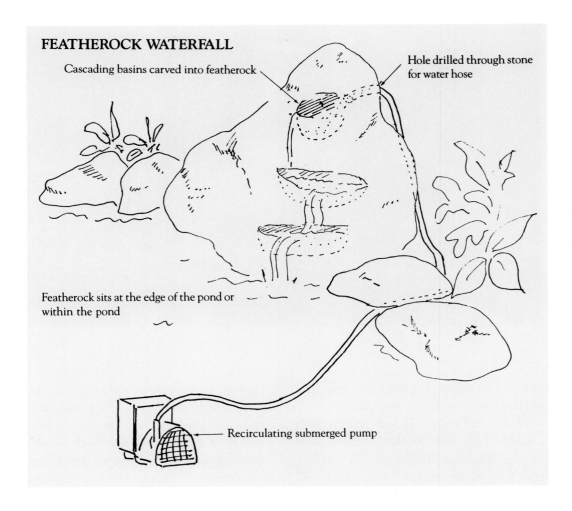

FEATHEROCK WATERFALL

Cascading basins carved into featherock

Hole drilled through stone for water hose

Featherock sits at the edge of the pond or within the pond

Recirculating submerged pump

STREAM COURSES

Stream courses are a variation of the waterfall construction. However, the longer the stream course, the more possibility of variety—a short series of waterfalls, occasional small pond areas, an island in the stream, and bog plantings. The stream is constructed in a series of level sections connected to lower areas via falls with the overall stream area smaller than its pond source. If it is necessary to top off the pond reservoir to start the stream moving, the bottom pond will flood when the pump is shut down.

A naturally appearing stream course fol-lows nature's guidelines—running in valleys, meandering around rock outcroppings, tumbling through narrow channels, and opening into calm pools. Natural streams have gently sloped sides, while canals have high, raised banks enclosing the waters. The hose that carries the water from the bottom pond to the top of the stream should be buried to the top of the stream, where it is made to appear to flow from a rock grotto.

Because the longer the stream section, the deeper the top end of that section must be, it is less trouble to excavate the stream as a series of short sections. Vary these

A meandering, lined stream is edged with various sizes of stones.

Photo courtesy of Maryland Aquatic Nurseries

sections to create interest and variety in the feature. Dig each section in the same manner as an informal, lined-pond construction. Close attention to the levels of each section ensures that the water flows through the course in the center of the bed. The water should attain a two-inch depth before tumbling into the next stream section. Using a level, establish the two-inch depth at the spillway end of a section so that it is below the surrounding ground level. Then, work back up the section to establish the depth for the water's entry into the section so it is the same level upon entry and exit. The section may be at its deepest at the head of the section.

The type of stream course being constructed determines the shaping of the excavation. Dig a stream meandering through a grassy area as a shallow "V." Rock-lined streams will be excavated as a straight-sided "U" so the rocks can be stacked upon each other to lead from the

Richard Schuck's lined stream includes bog plantings.

Photo courtesy of Maryland Aquatic Nurseries

A lined, natural pond recycles water through a water courseway and small falls.

Photo by Richard Schmitz

STREAM BED CONSTRUCTION

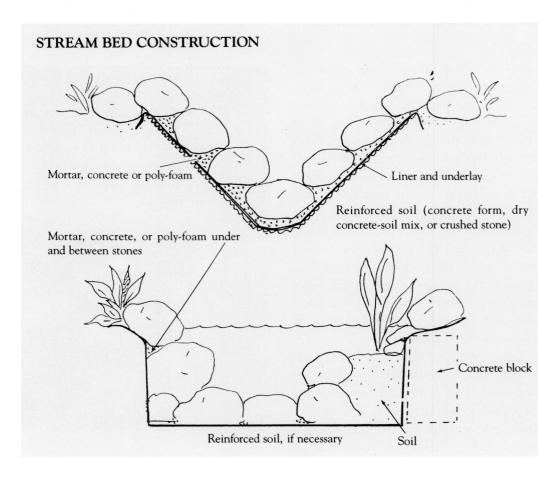

Mortar, concrete or poly-foam

Liner and underlay

Reinforced soil (concrete form, dry concrete-soil mix, or crushed stone)

Mortar, concrete, or poly-foam under and between stones

Concrete block

Reinforced soil, if necessary

Soil

stream to the bank. A bog-type stream excavation combines a planting-shelf area on the perimeter of a deeper, rock-lined area through which the water runs. Before determining the depth of the excavation, experiment with piles of rocks to estimate the depth needed to accommodate a particular design.

CONCRETE STREAM COURSES

Constructing the stream base of concrete can be challenging in frost-prone zones. Greater stability of the concrete is achieved if the course sections are kept short. Whatever the climate zone, follow the recommendations for thickness and reinforcement suggested by local building supply stores. Fully line the excavation beneath the concrete, following the same construction procedure outlined in Chapter Two for concrete collars and footings. If the sides of

the excavation are kept very gently sloped, forms other than the excavation itself may not have to be used.

Concrete blocks on a poured concrete base can be used for the side construction. Nine-inch concrete blocks are a good height as well as a good length for short sections. (See Chapter Five to adapt concrete block wall construction.)

Cut a "U"-shaped excavation to provide enough depth for the constructed form and its crushed stone underlay, approximately three to six inches, plus six inches for rocks in the bed, plus as much as 12 inches for planting shelves to put several inches of soil on. Each section should be constructed in its entirety at one time. The end of the section, where the water will spill over to the next, should be approximately three inches below the rest of the rim to allow for the flow. If plant shelves are desired, the width of the stream section could be approximately three feet across. Otherwise, the excavation will be 12 to 18 inches across. While the concrete is still wet, use a wire brush to roughen the spillway area and the entire bottom of the construction.

No rocks should be set directly into the concrete form. Once the concrete has set

A natural drainage ditch is lined with concrete and edged with stone to create a stream.

Photo by Joe Cook

A concrete stream flows gently through a backyard setting.

Photo by H. Nash

sufficiently, soft concrete can be applied to a roughened spillway area so flat spillway rocks can be pressed to the necessary level and angle. Mortar in place rockwork that will be incorporated in the spillway area to prevent water from running underneath.

Likewise, unless the water has a strong, ample flow through the stream course, it is likely to run under rather than over any stones put loosely into the stream bed. This is especially true if the pond reservoir is small. Since the bottom of the construction was roughened while the concrete was still wet, a thin layer of concrete or mortar will affix the bed stones. Use mortar between them as necessary. Create a plant shelf along the sides by cementing in four- to six-inch rocks along the edge to contain the soil.

Once the cementing is completed, cure, render, waterproof, and neutralize the entire structure before introducing the loose stones and soil in the planting area. (Cover the soil with a two-inch layer of pea gravel and assorted smaller rocks to contain the soil after planting.)

A lined stream wanders through a xeriscape of stone and Southwestern plants.

Photo by T.J. Smith

LINED WATER COURSE

Because stream courses are more vulnerable than a self-enclosed pond, use the strongest, most flexible liner available—butyl or EPDM. These liners can move better with the slight shifts in the ground and are easier to work with than stiffer materials.

Excavate the entire stream bed construction to the dimensions and shape, either a "V" or a "U," that is required for the design. As with the concrete construction, plan the course in short sections incorporating various widths, short waterfalls, and perhaps small bogs pooling below falls. Each section should incorporate the principles discussed above regarding depth of the heading and spillway of the falls. If the sections are kept relatively straight, less liner-folding will be required. If rocks are not affixed to the liner, folds should face the opposite direction of the water flow to avoid slowing it down.

Areas of the courseway to support heavy stones should be reinforced beneath the liner either with concrete pads or with several inches of crushed stone. Spillways especially require such reinforcement.

Begin constructing the courseway one section at a time, beginning at the bottom level that empties into the pond. The excavated section should be well-compacted, brushed free of loose soil and any sharp stones, and covered with at least an inch of moistened sand. Be sure to use an underlay fabric, too, for extra liner protection. Fit the liner piece into the excavated section, making certain the pond-edge-side overlaps generously into the pond. Arrange the folds in the liner to effect a fit and anchor the sides with stones temporarily. Arrange the spillway stones and affix with mortar or poly foam. Flat stones or small cobbles may also be affixed to the bed.

Moving to the next section, follow the same procedure as with the first. The liner should overlap the first section with enough length to be well anchored by stones. Cut off the underlay fabric at the spillway edge to prevent capillary seepage. Set the spillway stones before moving up to the next section. When the courseway is completed, create a camouflaged entry for the hose. If the hose is to be brought up alongside the stream, bury it before adding the final edging rocks.

As with a waterfall, bring up the liner behind the edge stonework to prevent water loss. Then embed the membrane in soil or hide it with more rocks.

Set the stones in mortar or concrete, or affix them with spray poly foam. (See Lined Waterfall Construction, this chapter.)

Large and small cobblestones are mortared over the liner to create a natural effect.

Photo by Eamonn Hughes

TIP

Obtain extra strength in concreting by using a concrete mix with added fiberglass particles. Camouflage the concrete by adding powdered color to the mix.

Timber accents a stream by embedding the wood in pads of concrete.

Photo by Greg Maxwell

Flexible forms line a stream bed being added to a pond.

Photo by Greg Maxwell

A dirt-and-concrete mix creates a solid stream wall behind the wooden form.

Photo by Greg Maxwell

The forms removed, concrete reinforced backfilling completes the stream preparation.

Photo by Greg Maxwell

The liner is fitted into the form and rocks are arranged to create a natural look.

Photo by Greg Maxwell

PREFORMED STREAM COURSES

Excavation is performed in a series of level steps, starting at the bottom where the stream will enter into the pond. As with a preformed waterfall, each section should overlap the lower. The excavated site is well-compacted, reinforced with crushed stone if necessary, and covered with a two-inch layer of sand. Be certain no sharp stones are present that might damage the form.

To position each section, use a spirit level and a straightedge to verify that the spillway is at the lowest point of each section. The spillway area should be two to three inches lower than the rest of the rim.

Flat stones or concrete pads help support the spillway area of each level of construction.

Use a hose as you proceed to be sure each level is properly set. Backfill with soil or sand and camouflage with rocks and planting pockets when the course is completed. Creeping and trailing plants are especially effective to conceal the edges, as are daylilies and ornamental grasses.

Pebbles are mortared onto the stream liner for a special effect.

Photo by Greg Maxwell

Chapter Nine
POND EDGINGS

The first consideration in choosing pond edging is the overall design of the pond and the yard. Formal designs rely on the harmony and stability of strict geometric shapes. Stone slabs, granite, slate, bricks, or same-size cobblestones work well. An informal pond can have turf or bog edging, as well as fieldstone, flat stones, bricks, or wood.

Another factor in making an edging choice is its function. Will there be foot traffic on the edging? Will people want to sit on the edge? Even if people aren't meant to stand on the edge, it may be wisest to construct your edging with standing in mind—for safety's sake. Even though many pond kits come with directions showing a simple placement of loose or stacked stones around the pond, such edgings can be precarious.

Provide reinforcement, too, for any weight, as rain-soaked ground will cause uneven settling of stones over time. In the case of light stonework, a few inches of crushed stone may be sufficient, as would a thin layer of concrete or stiff concrete worked into the top few inches of soil.

Large boulders set into the surrounding area create a natural appearance.

Photo by Richard Schmitz

Small plants are effectively planted in pockets of soil around the pond edge.

Photo by T.J. Smith

Pond Edgings 93

Stone rubble stacks easily and creates an informal, yet manicured, edge.

Photo by H. Nash

Concrete collars are often recommended for steep-sided ponds, as well as for ponds using heavy stonework. Likewise, plastic preformed ponds that require the edging to rest primarily on the surrounding ground to avoid collapsing the side walls may need a concrete-reinforced perimeter.

Avoid selecting soft rocks that crumble easily. Although less expensive, they begin deteriorating in a short time, producing unsafe conditions and leaching excess minerals into the water.

Put a gap in concrete ponds between the pond walls and the edging to avoid winter cracking where the pond water expands at a faster rate than the pond itself. A thin layer of plastic sheeting with the edging mortared onto it and the bulk of the edging weight resting on the surrounding ground will work.

Remember, mortar does not bond well to liner materials. It is important that the foundation in the adjacent ground adequately support and anchor the edging.

Whatever the edging choice, if mortar or concrete is used, be sure to waterproof it or treat it for lime. A good period of rainy weather may result in excessively high pH levels in the pond.

Unless the pond is large enough to accommodate gently sloped sides to the desired maximum depth, the side walls must be practically vertical. Vertical sides allow the liner to be better concealed by the slightly extended coping. (See Chapter 2 for establishing a sharp pond edge.)

Before starting the edge construction, use a spirit level and straight edge both around the pond perimeter as well as across its width and length. Be certain the pond is completely level. Remember to plan for space in the edging for electric cables and waterfall hoses, if necessary.

Bring up the liner behind the edging to prevent surface runoffs from flooding the pond, as well as to help prevent pond overflow. Sloping the edging slightly down and away from the pond helps prevent runoff contamination. Also, having the pond edge set a few inches above the surrounding grade is an adequate deterrent in low-to-normal rainfall areas. Set the pond edge four inches above the existing grade in rainy areas. (See drainage options in Chapter Two.) Backfill the area behind the liner edge with soil, stone, mulch, or sodded turf.

FORMAL EDGINGS

Formal ponds look best with the water level at or just below the edging. This effect, called brimming, requires an absolutely level capstone. Mortar used for setting the edging should be thin at the pond edge so it is not conspicuously visible. Additional stability is granted by increasing the mor-

tar thickness towards the back of the edging, but do not tilt the edging in towards the pond at ground level.

PAVED EDGING

Paving is heavy. A concrete collar provides the best support for this type of edging, although a single layer of paving may be adequately secured upon a several-inch layer of crushed stone.

The paving slabs should be embedded in mortar for stability. Because smaller pavers can be tilted by a person's weight, use larger slabs where people are likely to stand. Likewise, the slabs should be large enough to overhang the pond by an inch or two.

Small cobbles can line a gently sloped pond and be extended up out of the water to form the pond edge.

Photo by Greg Jones

Building the pond first and then constructing the deck around it is the easiest way for in-deck pond construction.

Photo by Greg Maxwell

The completed decking offers close viewing and enjoyment of the pond.

Photo by Greg Maxwell

TIP

Scott Bates recommends embedding rock edgings in a concrete mix:

2 shovelsful portland cement

4 shovelsful Mason/sharp sand

1 shovelful Swift Set™

2 shovelsful pea gravel

Mix with water and Fortifier Acrylic™ bonding agent (mixed 1 qt. to 5 gal. water). This technique allows facing the liner from a shallow shelf up over the pond edge.

BRICK EDGING

Bricks offer a variety of choices in pond-edging material and can be used for both formal and informal ponds. Single brick edging does not require any great reinforcement for support; a few inches of crushed stone is usually sufficient. Because bricks cannot be mortared to liner material securely, some sort of stable surround should be provided for their anchoring.

An interesting variation on the use of bricks is to mortar stacked bricks onto the liner from the planting shelf up to the ground level where the edging row is constructed. Perfectly level shelves are required for this construction.

It is best to avoid using bricks with holes as they invite grass and weeds, besides cracking and crumbling in freezing climates. Engineering bricks—the thin, solid pavers designed for outdoor use—can be used as an edging and also extended into a paved area surrounding the pond.

In using bricks as an edging for the pre-formed pond, the weight of the bricks should rest predominantly on the surrounding ground—just in case somebody chooses to stand on them. The water level of the pond should be maintained below the brick edging since a waterproof bond cannot be established between the pond and the bricks with mortar.

Bricks used as an edging for a concrete pond can be mortared directly to the pond walls. However, to allow for expansion, they shouldn't be mortared into any surrounding paving.

ROCK EDGING

Rocks are probably the most commonly used pond edgings, and the most commonly misused edgings. It's very easy to string them around the pond perimeter and create the traditional "rock necklace." But a little variation in rock sizes and random nearby placements achieves a natural appearance.

STONE EDGING

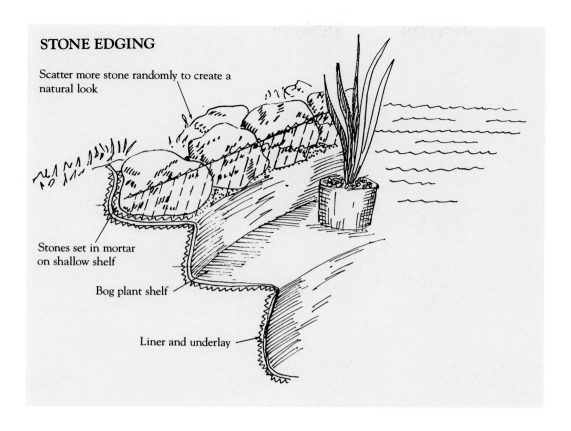

Scatter more stone randomly to create a
natural look

Stones set in mortar
on shallow shelf

Bog plant shelf

Liner and underlay

BOULDER EDGING

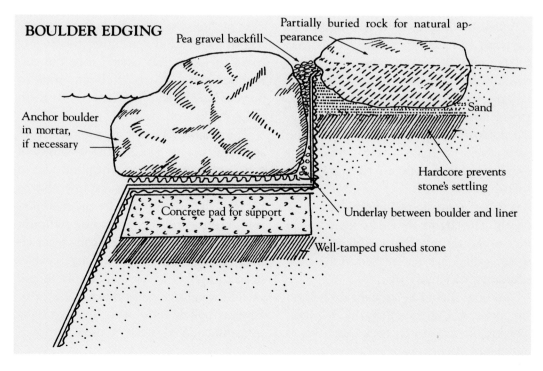

Pea gravel backfill

Partially buried rock for natural appearance

Anchor boulder
in mortar,
if necessary

Sand

Hardcore prevents
stone's settling

Concrete pad for support

Underlay between boulder and liner

Well-tamped crushed stone

Large boulders and featherock combine to create the edge of this garden.

Photo by H. Nash

A well-reinforced, shallow shelf around the pond can support stacked rocks that spill out into the surrounding ground, with various sizes providing interest. A large rock can peek through the water. Smaller rocks can fill between larger ones. An added benefit of such a construction is the water-access provided to birds. An extra layer of padding between the rocks and liner should be used.

It is best to avoid laying the pond edge loosely. The edging should be set in a concrete or mortar mix that is well supported by several inches of crushed stone or a substantial concrete collar.

The liner should be brought up behind the rocks and anchored by more rocks, concrete, or substantial backfilling of soil and plants. Stones scattered about appear most natural when they seem to be embedded in soil. Avoid cementing the edging rocks to rocks that extend into the surrounding area in a cold climate zone to prevent undesirable, additional stress on the pond walls.

The main problem with using rocks or stones as pond edging is the difficulty of getting them to overhang the pond edge to provide sun protection to the liner. Rocks big enough to do this may be out of proportion to the pond size. Providing sufficient reinforcement beneath them can create additional work and expense. Large cobbles or fieldstone, however, can be split in half or lightweight, reconstituted stone or fiberglass hollow rocks with lips that hang over the pond edge can be used.

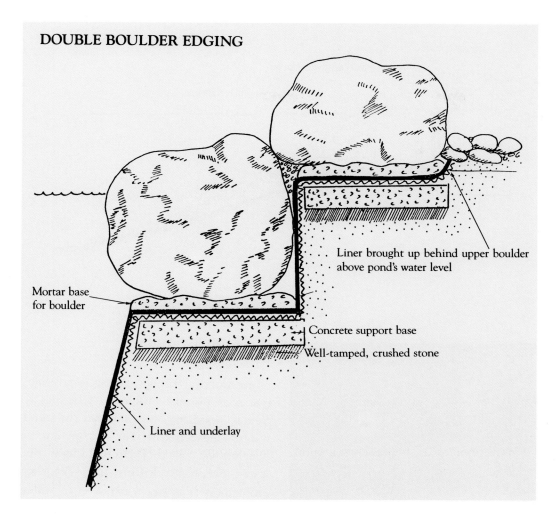

DOUBLE BOULDER EDGING

Liner brought up behind upper boulder above pond's water level

Mortar base for boulder

Concrete support base

Well-tamped, crushed stone

Liner and underlay

GRAVEL AND PEBBLE EDGING

A larger pond can be edged with gravel or pebbles. Even if this method is used in only one section of the pond, the birds that visit the pond to bathe and drink will be grateful. Naturally, this edging treatment is informal. The biggest problem with this type of edging is the silt, debris, and algae that may accumulate in the gravel. Cleaning the gravel is usually required every couple of years. Sharp, angular gravel should be avoided and liner protection provided if it is likely anybody may walk upon the gravel.

The lined pond requires that the liner be brought up above the pond's water level and then buried back into the surrounding soil into a trench of sorts, the "trench" being filled with pea gravel or other suitable small stone. The gravel then extends from shallow water up onto the dry land. A submerged stone wall can also be built upon a planting ledge, the area behind it backfilled with the gravel. The natural look of the pebbled beach can be extended into the pond itself by covering the bottom of the pond with an inch or two of the same pebbles. Added advantages of this construction are the foraging area provided for

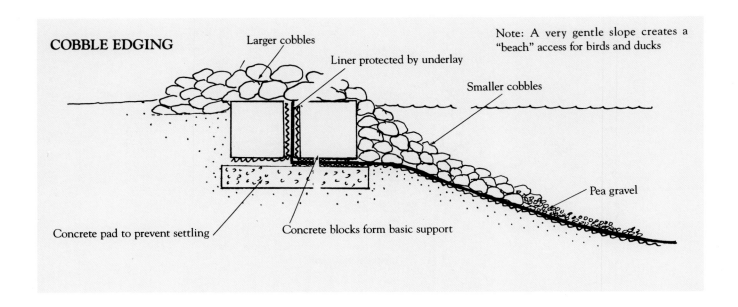

COBBLE EDGING

Larger cobbles

Liner protected by underlay

Note: A very gentle slope creates a "beach" access for birds and ducks

Smaller cobbles

Pea gravel

Concrete pad to prevent settling

Concrete blocks form basic support

The use of cobbles and stone along with a shallow bog area creates a natural pond.

Photo by Eamonn Hughes

fish, a medium for the growth of submerged plants, and the concealment of particulate matter that settles on the pond bottom.

Fixed-form ponds such as preforms or concrete forms can include pebbled beaches by the same backfill method. If the planting shelf is too narrow to support a stone wall, dark colored engineering bricks may be used.

WOOD EDGING

Using wood or timber edging is possible, but does present problems. Chemically treated wood may contaminate the pond water. These toxins may not be immediately toxic, but they can build up in the water, eventually killing fish. Another problem is that wood exposed to water tends to warp and rot. Because of this, they shouldn't be permanently affixed to the pond.

Wood edging, however, can be nailed to a fiberglass support plate that is installed in a groove around the pond's edge. It may also be affixed to a wall or concrete support with stainless steel straps.

Short timbers of varied heights can be embedded in a layer of concrete set on a shallow shelf around the pond. Bring the liner up behind the timber edging and secure it over concrete haunches or stones and bury it in soil. Bring turf or decorative gravel to the edge.

If the feeling of wood or timber is de-

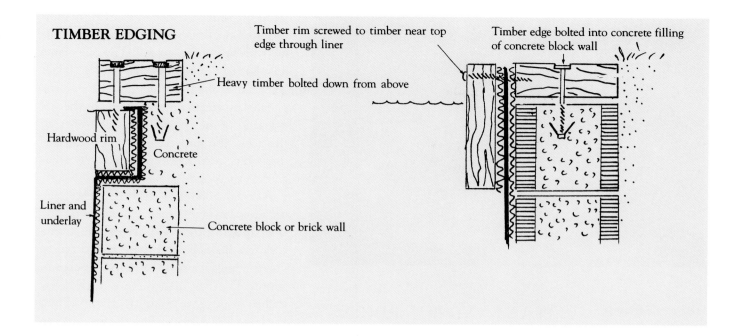

TIMBER EDGING

Timber rim screwed to timber near top edge through liner

Heavy timber bolted down from above

Hardwood rim

Concrete

Liner and underlay

Concrete block or brick wall

Timber edge bolted into concrete filling of concrete block wall

---

sired, consider concrete structures that look like logs and wood. Treated properly for lime, such products may achieve the desired appearance with a longer life than real wood.

TURF EDGING

Turf or grassy edgings are particularly appropriate to informal and wildlife ponds. They do require a ban on the nearby use of lawn chemicals and a tender hand with the mowing. Grass blown into the pond produces a mess and can result in thick, green water. It may be necessary to cut the pond-edge grass by hand.

LineUps™ facilitate this type of edge construction. (See Chapter 2.) Similar constructions can be made of wood forms or the liner sharply dipped back into the soil over a concrete haunch.

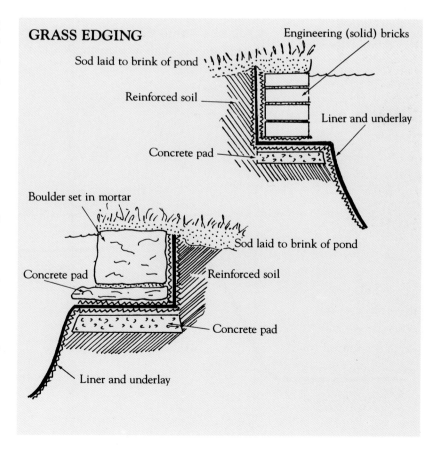

GRASS EDGING

Engineering (solid) bricks

Sod laid to brink of pond

Reinforced soil

Liner and underlay

Concrete pad

Boulder set in mortar

Concrete pad

Sod laid to brink of pond

Reinforced soil

Concrete pad

Liner and underlay

The turf edging is slightly elevated to prevent surface runoff contamination.

Photo courtesy of Charleston Aquatic Nurseries

PLANT AND BOG EDGING

One of the most natural ways to edge an informal pond is with plant or bog gardens. A bog area within the pond is easily constructed on the shallow planting ledge. A retaining wall is created by stacking or mortaring stone, bricks, or blocks and backfilling with heavy garden soil. The bog plants are planted directly into the soil.

Because small water gardens can be plagued by green-water problems as the soil nutrients of the bog garden leach back into the pond, the garden can also be created as a separate construction immediately adjacent to the pond.

A lined pond can easily accommodate an adjacent bog garden by extending the liner up above the pond's water level, over a concrete haunch, and then back down to create a bog area of up to 16 to 18 inches in depth. The bog area is lined with a few inches of pea gravel and then soil. Plant the bog plants directly into the soil and top with an inch or so of pea gravel. Any overflow of the pond can then be directed into the bog garden by having the pond edging in that area set slightly lower than the edge

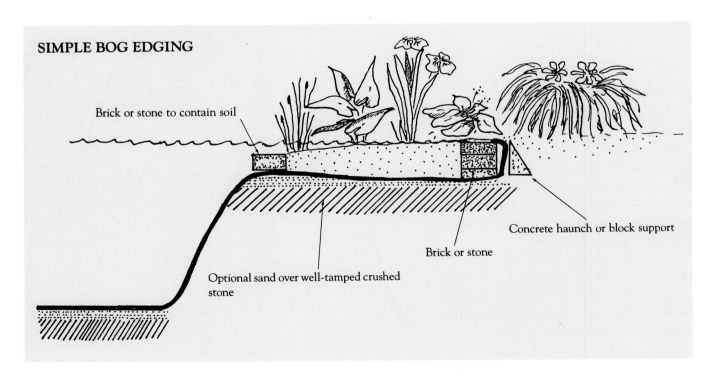

SIMPLE BOG EDGING

Brick or stone to contain soil

Concrete haunch or block support

Brick or stone

Optional sand over well-tamped crushed stone

of the rest of the pond.

A perforated tube or hose, sunk into the bog garden when it is constructed, can keep the bog from drying out. Seal the downward end of the hose and affix a plug to the upper end. During dry spells, a hose can be attached to the unplugged end and water added without disturbing the soil's surface.

ADDING A BOG GARDEN

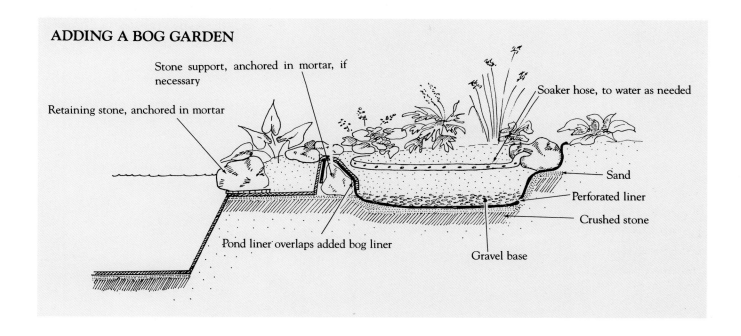

Stone support, anchored in mortar, if necessary

Retaining stone, anchored in mortar

Soaker hose, to water as needed

Pond liner overlaps added bog liner

Sand

Perforated liner

Crushed stone

Gravel base

NATURAL POND EDGING

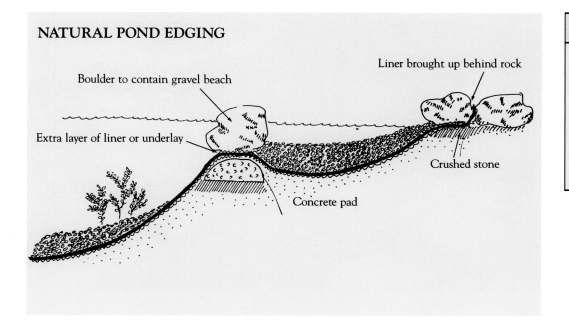

Boulder to contain gravel beach

Liner brought up behind rock

Extra layer of liner or underlay

Crushed stone

Concrete pad

TIP

A separate, lined bog garden should have its liner perforated to prevent stagnant water from collecting in it.

Chapter Ten
PUMPS AND FILTRATION

PUMPS AND MECHANICAL FILTRATION

Although a clear water garden is possible without the use of a pump or filtration system if the pond is kept clean, the number of fish is kept within the recommended stocking rate, and the pond has enough submerged grasses, most water gardens use recirculating water. With the growing popularity of water gardening, many new pump and filtration developments are appearing in the market place. Most notable, perhaps, is the almost exclusive use of submersible pumps, now manufactured in black to blend into the bottom of the pond against a black liner.

In the past, many pump housings were made of aluminum alloys. Because aluminum oxidizes in pond water, such pumps need a sacrificial anode attached to the pump. The anode oxidizes first, so it, rather than an expensive pump, is replaced. Stainless steel, brass, or plastic housings will not oxidize in pond water. The only oxidation precaution with these pumps is to not use two dissimilar metals in close proximity within the pond; the softer metal will oxidize.

Even though many authorities still recommend turning the pond water over within a specific time-frame, a clean, ecologically-balanced pond does not require rigid management. Except in very small ponds, water flow can be based on the requirements of the water feature.

Fountain assemblies and additional filtration units may be attached to the submersible pump.
Photo courtesy of Rena Corporation

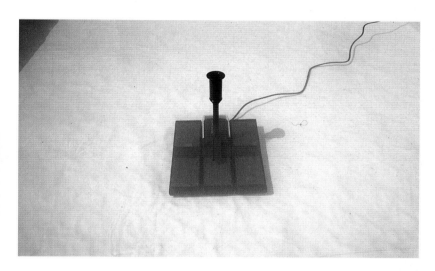

Pump size is generally calculated based on the gallons per hour output at one foot of lift or height. Most manufacturers offer a chart that shows the GPH at additional incremental increases. An additional factor to consider is the length of hosing from the pump to the water feature. For every ten feet of hosing, resistance within the hose produces a decrease in output of one foot of lift. (See Appendix for pump chart and recommended hosing sizes.)

To prevent oxidation of aluminum housings, a sacrificial anode is attached to the pump.
Photo courtesy of Little Giant Pump Corporation

An aquarium-type undergravel filtration system produces sparkling, clear water.

Photo by Lee Dreyfuss

TIP

For a quick estimate of the pumping needs at a one-foot height, add two zeros to the inch width of the spillway.

Hidden plumbwork does not detract from the pond's aesthetics.

Photo by Lee Dreyfuss

Many pumps are equipped with a small particulate filter to prevent debris from entering the pump.

Photo by Oliver Jackson, courtesy of Custom Fountains

To determine the pump size required, fill a five-gallon bucket with water and experiment with its flow over the waterfall. Determine how many seconds it takes to achieve the desired appearance, divide 60 seconds in a minute by that number of seconds, and multiply by five. This will give the number of gallons per minute needed for the desired look. Multiply this figure by 60, to determine the number of gallons per hour required. Figure the height of the waterfall lift, plus any adjustments for the length of hosing, and compare the desired GPH with the pump chart to determine exactly what size pump is needed. (A one-foot high waterfall with a six-inch wide spillway would require a 600 GPH pump, for example. Increasing the spillway to 20 inches wide would require a pump of approximately 2000 GPH.)

Generally, the size of hosing used from the pump should be the next size up from the diameter of the pump outlet. This will require an adapter which should be affixed with stainless steel clamps. The larger the hose diameter, the more gentle the flow. If the flow is too strong, increasing the hose diameter may produce the desired effect.

Restrictor clamps can make minor adjustments in water flow. The clamps must be affixed to the discharge hose of the pump to prevent stressing and burning the pump. A tee connection avoids clamps and diverts some of the water to another water feature, such as a spouting ornament or a small fountain.

Most pumps have a screen apparatus over the pump's intake to keep out debris and baby fish or tadpoles. These screens may clog and stress the pump during the spring and autumn months. A 200 GPH pump, for example, needs approximately 40 square inches of screening. Wrapping the pump in fiberglass screen gives more particulate filtration. Larger filter box assemblies are readily available, too. Hose the debris from the screen of the assembly, and rinse the foam media inside, as needed.

Lighting the pond area allows nighttime enjoyment of the pond.

Photo courtesy of Reimer Waterscapes

Electricity

Electricity and water are a dangerous combination. Never use an extension cord to the pond. Many local ordinances require the use of a licensed electrician for any installation work; check the regulations before starting construction.

Outlets should be at least four feet from the pond and housed in waterproof casings. Protect the entire circuit with a ground fault circuit interrupter. A lock on the cord to prevent any inadvertent disconnection is advisable.

The main electrical cable should be armored and buried at the depth specified by local ordinances. Cable over 100 feet will have a significant drop in voltage. A pump can be plugged into a lighting outlet, but should be separately switched and fused; this requires at least a four-core armored cable.

If a slight tingling is felt in the pond water or if the fish are unduly agitated and jumping, turn off the electricity and check the system.

Generally, the smaller the pond, the more likely a recirculating pump is needed. Although fish do get most of their oxygen from water surface exchange, a small pond may require supplemental aeration from a pump.

Underwater lights bring a glow to a pond, waterfall, or fountain display.

Photo courtesy of Little Giant Pump Corporation

Surface Skimming Filtration

Many years ago, Joe B. Dekker of Aquascape Designs in Wycliff, New Jersey, designed a pond filtration system based on the surface skimming filtration systems used in swimming pools. It is most effective in ponds of at least 4 × 6 feet and with submersible water garden pumps producing at least 750 gallons per hour.

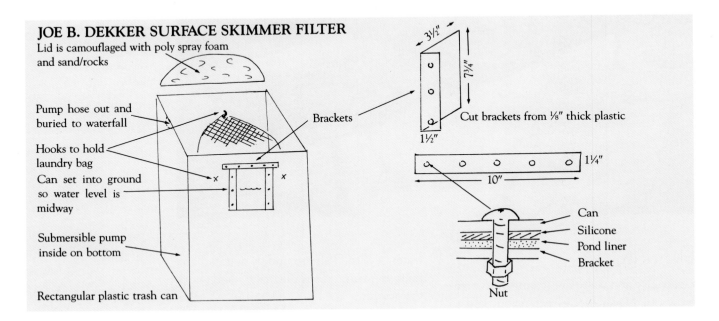

JOE B. DEKKER SURFACE SKIMMER FILTER

Lid is camouflaged with poly spray foam and sand/rocks

Pump hose out and buried to waterfall

Hooks to hold laundry bag

Can set into ground so water level is midway

Submersible pump inside on bottom

Rectangular plastic trash can

Brackets

3½"

7¾"

1½"

Cut brackets from ⅛" thick plastic

1¼"

10"

Can
Silicone
Pond liner
Bracket

Nut

Materials Needed

One 30 gallon, heavy-duty, plastic trash can

one 10 × 9 inch piece of plastic, ⅛ inch thick

11 ⁶/₃₂–1¼ inch bolts with nuts

5 screw-in hooks

one tube of RTV single-component silicone

one nylon mesh laundry bag

1¼ inch flexible black hosing to reach from pump to waterfall

submersible water garden pump of at least 750 GPH

hose adapter for hosing, if required

optional: filter foam to fit inside dimension of trash can, spray foam for camouflaging lid

The return water from the skimmer filtration system is routed through a Bio Falls Filter™ to keep the pond water sparkling clean.

Photo by Gary G. Wittstock

A surface skimmer filtration system promotes clear water by preventing floating organic matter from dirtying the water.

Photo by Gary G. Wittstock

With the lid and stone cover removed, the CleanSweep Skimmer™ is readily accessible for service.

Photo by Gary G. Wittstock

Construction Procedure

Preliminaries

1. Excavate a hole adjacent to the pond edge to accommodate a 30-gallon, heavy-duty, plastic trash can so the pond's water level will be at the mid-point of the centered 7 × 8 inch cut-out 1½ inches from the top of the can.
2. Layer the bottom of the excavation with 2 to 4 inches of well-tamped, crushed stone.
3. Provide a shallow trench from the can to the waterfall for routing the flexible return hosing.

Preparing the can:

1. Mark and cut out a 7 (vertical) × 8 (horizontal) inch rectangle 1½ inches down from the top and centered on the front of the can.
2. Cut a slot from the top edge for the pump hose and electrical cord to exit the can above the water level when the lid is replaced.
3. Cut brackets from ⅛ inch thick plastic:
   One at 10 × 1¼ inches
   Two at 7 × 1¼ inches
4. Set the can into the prepared excavation.
5. Apply a ¼ × ½ inch line of RTV single-component silicone around the face of the can's cut-out. Press the pond liner to the can face and hold it firmly to the silicone by bolting on the three brackets. Brackets and can edges should be predrilled. (The silicone will require a minimum of 24 hours to cure before water can be run through it.)
6. Use the can's cut-out as a guide to cut the liner across the top and down the sides for a matching hole. Fold the liner flap to the inside of the can.
7. Attach two screw-in hooks approximately eight inches down from the top of the can on each side of the cut-out and two screw-in hooks one inch down from the top of the can on each side of the cut-out. Attach another hook one inch down, to the center of the opposite side of the can. The laundry bag will hang from the five hooks with the pond liner flap within the bag.
8. Connect the flexible hosing to the pump and place the pump in the bottom of the can. Route the hosing and pump's electrical cord from the can.
9. Optional foam may be cut to fit inside the can over the pump for additional small-particle filtration.
10. Attach the edge of the mesh bag onto the hooks while keeping the slack to a minimum.
11. Spray foam may be sprayed onto the can lid and sand tossed onto it for camouflage. Flat paving stones can also be used to hide the lid.

Using the Skimmer Filter

1. During operation, maintain the water level at one-half to one-third the way up the opening of the cut-out.
2. Clean out the nylon bag as needed. Hose clean any foam media as needed.

BIO-FILTRATION

Bio-filtration makes use of nitrifying bacteria to change organic wastes and ammonia into nitrite and then into nitrates. Since the bacteria need moving water and oxygen to survive, it is necessary to use a water feature and/or a natural filtration system such as Richard Schuck's Ten Percent Solution.

The water in ponds for special fish, such as koi or exotic goldfish or in ponds that are maximally stocked with fish, may require the extra attention to quality a bio-filter offers. Manufacturers now market filters with submersible, in-pond designs. These systems are restricted to smaller ponds under 1,200 gallons.

Larger ponds that need bio-filtration use external constructions; pond water is

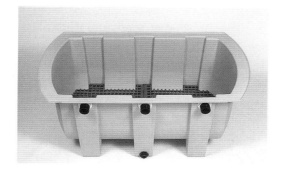

A bio-filter container is fitted with an inside grill to hold various media.

Photo courtesy of Maryland Aquatic Nurseries

Lava rock, washed clean, is an excellent bio-filter medium.

Photo courtesy of Maryland Aquatic Nurseries

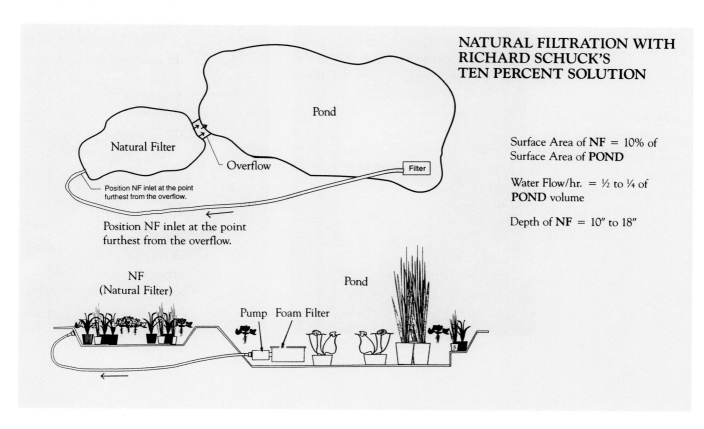

NATURAL FILTRATION WITH RICHARD SCHUCK'S TEN PERCENT SOLUTION

Pond

Natural Filter

Overflow

Position NF inlet at the point furthest from the overflow.

Position NF inlet at the point furthest from the overflow.

NF (Natural Filter)

Pump Foam Filter

Pond

Surface Area of **NF** = 10% of Surface Area of **POND**

Water Flow/hr. = ½ to ¼ of **POND** volume

Depth of **NF** = 10″ to 18″

pumped into a series of chambers for mechanical filtration of debris and particulate matter and bio-filtration by the nitrifying bacteria growing on various media forms.

The key to such out-of-pond systems is the rate water flows through them. Since the first chamber is designed to collect particulate matter, the water must flow at a rate that allows the particles to settle within the chamber, ideally one gallon per minute per square foot of chamber area. If space is a problem, baffles or brushes can be added to slow the water movement through this chamber. Site the intake hosing to this initial chamber in the upper third of the tank. Clean this chamber frequently to lessen the bio-load on the rest of the system.

Henry and Carole Reimer of Reimer Waterscapes in Canada report a simple, but effective, bio-filter. Inside the pond, set up a 200 to 500 GPH pump with an attached particle filter on the water intake. Have a one-half inch hose lead out of the pond and into a half 45-gallon drum container. Fill the drum with one-inch diameter polyethylene pipe cut into two-inch long segments. Predator netting can also be used in place of the pipe pieces. Silicone a 1½ inch PVC pipe into the upper side of the drum to allow the water's return to the pond. Use a solid cover to keep out sunlight. This system can be camouflaged in the back of a waterfall.

External bio-filters are stacked out of view.

Photo by H. Nash

Bio-filtration systems are recommended for ponds with a maximum fish load.

Photo by H. Nash

NATURAL FILTRATION

1

3

2

4

5

Preformed natural filter containers allow the water to flow from them.

Photo courtesy of Maryland Aquatic Nurseries

Four natural filters are set up with plants to naturally filter the recycled pond water.

Photo courtesy of Maryland Aquatic Nurseries

The same bio-filters display the lush growth of only three weeks.

Photo courtesy of Maryland Aquatic Nurseries

A wooden enclosure conceals the natural filters.

Photo courtesy of Maryland Aquatic Nurseries

Water celery or other aquatics grown in the top of a bio-filter provide extra natural filtration.

Photo courtesy of Maryland Aquatic Nurseries

Chapter Eleven
OTHER WATER FEATURES

Water will flow the strongest through the jet nearest the intake valve or through the straightest pipe.

Several fountains set up within a pond can be operated from a single large-diameter pipe that runs the full length of the features. Smaller pipes connecting from the main pipe then share even pressure.

Small-holed jets can clog and require cleaning. A good mechanical particulate filter attached to the pump's intake will help. Since severe clogging stresses the pump, set it on a riser to prevent intake of dirty water from the pond bottom.

Plumbed statuary adds delightful aesthetics to a pond.

Photo courtesy of Florentine Craftsmen

FOUNTAINS

Water fountains provide both sound and movement in the water garden. They are best suited to the formal garden or to a fish pond since water lilies do not grow well when exposed to constant water movement or splashing by a fountain.

Keep surrounding landscapes simple and restrained for the most effective use of fountains. Tall vertical jets look best against a vertical backdrop, while low, arching jets look best with rounded shapes behind them.

Site fountains where wind will not scatter their spray. This can cause excessive water loss besides detracting from the fountain's appearance.

Although several jets can be operated by the same pump, affixing each jet to its own control valve controls their appearance.

An elevated basin fountain is the focal point of the formal pond at Mackinac Island's Grand Hotel.

Photo by H. Nash

Wall fountains can add a classical or whimsical touch to the pond.

Photo courtesy of Toscano

compacted. Placing them on concrete or flat-stone pavers provides stability.

Wall fountains offer an interesting water option. Water circulates from within a small basin by a tiny submersible pump through a spouting or overflowing ornament. These features can be mounted on a garden wall or on the back wall of a pond. Conceal the water delivery and electrical supplies for the fullest aesthetic enjoyment.

Fountain Basins and Wall Fountains

A plumbed hand pump provides moving water.

Photo by H. Nash

Fountains and piped statuary require only a basin or reservoir. A shallow basin at least as wide as the fountain easily holds and conceals a small pump. Maryland Aquatic Nurseries has developed a plastic basin fitted with a grating approximately two-thirds of the way up from the basin bottom. Lightweight decorative media, such as clay balls, cover the grating up to the edge of the basin. The basin is filled with water that recycles through a carved featherock. Plants grow hydroponically within the media; although the media may be attractive, the concept is safe for use around children.

Spouting statuary set within or attached to the sides of broad basins with a small pump concealed beneath the water allows enjoyment of the sound and movement of water. Floating aquatics, such as water hyacinth or water lettuce, may be grown in the basin.

The main concern with these types of water features is that their area is well-

STEPPING STONES IN THE POND

Stepping stones can be used in both formal and informal ponds. Stone squares that match or coordinate with the pond itself or long slabs bridging the water suit formal pond designs.

Informal ponds offer more freedom in

size and composition of stepping stones.

Since heavy stones exert weight on the pond bottom, suitable reinforcement should be provided in the pond base. Concrete pads or footing reinforcements beneath a liner or flat stones set upon protective pads on the liner serve to spread out the weight of pedestals and stepping stones.

Pedestals for stepping stones can be constructed of concrete blocks. If the stones will be walked on, it is advisable to mortar the blocks together for extra stability. The pedestals should raise the stepping stones an inch or two above the water level to prevent slippery algae growth. Any concrete or mortar work should be lime-neutralized.

Stepping-stones may be set directly on a shallow stream base.

Photo by H. Nash

A classic deer drip may be incorporated into a pond design or may stand alone.

Photo courtesy of Bamboo Fencer

A concrete and exposed aggregate walkover bridge was made with wooden forms.

Photo by H. Nash

A bridge crossing a small stream features hand railings for safety.

Photo by H. Nash

BRIDGES

For maximum effectiveness, place bridges where their use appears logical. Install adequate footings beyond the rim of the pond for maximum stability. Handrails should be located closely enough together that a small child cannot slip through.

If the bridge is constructed of wood, leave a slight gap of up to a quarter of an inch between each plank to prevent water from collecting and creating a slippery surface. The height should always be above the highest water level in the pond.

ISLANDS

Large concrete or lined ponds can include an island. Providing reinforced concrete footings under the liner or wide slabs on the pond bottom prevents damage to the pond membrane.

The island itself can be constructed of

concrete blocks. To counter water pressure, solid blocks should be used or the hollows filled with concrete. The blocks may be mortared together for stability. Render and treat the blocks for lime, perhaps with a black water sealant that will make the sides less conspicuous in the pond. Fill the interior of the island with soil and plant it. If the island is more than two feet deep, the bottom portion may be filled with rubble. Feature statuary or construct a waterfall on the island.

Another alternative is to use the island construction as a pond within a pond. Gaps may be left in the block-constructed wall so a pump can recirculate all the water. Paint the concrete blocks with black sealant. The inner pond may feature a fountain with the edging of the wall providing a waterfall effect. Koi ponds may grow water lilies in the inner pond, too.

A straight bridge-span is given character with stone facing.

Photo by Robert Johnson

A planter in the pond creates an island.

Photo by Robert Johnson

A water wheel creates a charming feature for the larger pond.

Photo by H. Nash

WHISKEY BARREL OR TUB GARDENS

Whiskey barrels, wine casks, or tub gardens can be used effectively as patio or lawn planters set above the ground or sunken within it. Such gardens set above-ground in cold climates need to winter the plants and fish indoors. A plastic tent allows their wintering over if the tubs are set in the ground. These small planters are especially useful for growing lotuses.

Whiskey barrels or wine casks must be lined to prevent leaching of tannic acid and alcohol residues that will kill fish and plants.

BOG GARDENS

Bog gardens are constructed in the same way as a lined pond. The excavation should be 18 inches deep and the liner set in over a layer of sand. The liner is punctured throughout the bottom for drainage. Up to four inches of crushed stone or pea gravel is placed in the garden and eight to 10 inches of soil filled on top. Edging is placed around the garden, bog plants set into the soil, and water added to the edging.

Bury a perforated hose in the soil with the end capped and the hose connected at the soil's surface for watering the garden as necessary. Control mosquitoes in shallow water with Mosquito Dunks™, floating bacteria that kill mosquito larvae.

APPENDIX 1

Dreams and Inspirations

Designed by Joe Scheidler, photo by T.J. Smith

Designed by Joe Scheidler, photo by T.J. Smith

Designed by Joe B. Dekker, photo by Joe B. Dekker

Designed by Eamonn Hughes,
photo by Eamonn Hughes

Designed by Kiyoshi Okuhara,
photo by H. Nash

Designed by Greg Jones,
photo by Greg Jones

A beautiful formal pond at Mt. Assisi Gardens, in Lovetto, Pennsylvania.

Photo by Roseanne Conrad

Designed by Cla Allgood,
photo by Cla Allgood

Designed by Post Landscape
Services, photo by Carol
Christensen

Designed by Richard
Schmitz, photo by Richard
Schmitz

Missouri Botanical Gardens,
photo by Greg Speichert

Designed by Richard
Schmitz, photo by Richard
Schmitz

APPENDIX 2

Plants for the Water Garden

Lotus, Chawan Basu

Photo by Greg Speichert/Crystal Palace Perennials

Nymphaea—Hardy water lilies are true perennials, experiencing winter dormancy. They can be wintered over in a pond provided the lily root does not freeze. Most water lilies require at least five hours of sunlight. The surface coverage, or spread, of a lily is generally twice its depth in the water. Dwarf and pygmy lilies require only 6–10 inches of water over the plant's crown. Medium-sized lilies require 10 to 20 inches, and large lilies do best with 16 to 32 inches of water over the crown. Hardy water lilies are available in white, pink, red, yellow, and changeables—generally yellow to bronze or red over the four-day life-span of the blossom. Their blooms open by mid-morning and close in the mid-to-late afternoon. A lily leaf's life span may be only two weeks in the summer, but others are produced throughout the season.

Sunshine Bush,
Ludwigia peruviana

Photo by Greg Speichert/Crystal Palace Perennials

Tropical water lilies require a minimum temperature of 70°F and above, lots of sunlight, and regular feeding for their profuse bloom. They usually hold their flowers well above the water and are available in a sparkling array of colors, including blues and purples. They require only 6–12 inches of water over the plant's crown. Like their hardy cousins, these lilies need at least five or six hours of sunlight daily, although some of the blues seem more tolerant of less. Day bloomers are open from mid-morning to mid-afternoon; night bloomers are open from late afternoon to mid-morning of the next day.

Lotus—Like hardy water lilies, lotuses are fully hardy so long as their tubers are not allowed to freeze. Standard-sized lotuses may grow to five feet, while dwarf forms may reach only three feet or less. Rampant growers, they need as large a pot as possible. Research suggests they need feeding only once or twice a season. They require temperatures above 80°F to flower, as well as long, sunny days.

Lilylike, deep-water aquatics

Aponogeton distachyus (Water Hawthorne)—Long, strap-like leaves float on the water surface with vanilla-scented, white, forked blossoms during early spring and late autumn. This hardy plant may go dormant in the heat of summer. Grows in 6–24 inches of water.

Hydrocleys nymphoides (Water Poppy)—Tropical, shiny ovate green leaves appear to be dwarfed water lily leaves. Flowers are three-petaled, papery, yellow poppies of brief life, but frequent bloom. Grown as an annual in temperate zones.

Nymphoides (Water Snowflakes, Fringed Water Snowflake, Floating Heart)—a group of tropical plants grown much like water lilies with floating leaves and short-lived yellow or white flowers, some varieties with fringed edges. The plants spread by long trailing runners that will root into other plant pots when available. The common yellow-flowering *peltata* (Floating Heart) is the only hardy one in the group. The others must be grown as annuals in temperate zones.

Marginal Plants

These plants may be grown with two to six inches of water over the plant crown on plant shelves or on pedestals within the water garden.

Acorus calamus (Sweet Flag, comes in variegated form, also)—Iris, straplike foliage with nondescript "flower." Grows 2–nearly 3 feet tall from a shallow-rooted, creeping rhizome that requires a broad-mouthed pot. Fully hardy in zone five with no special winter care.

Acorus gramineus ssp (Japanese dwarf sweet flag)—Available in cream or yellow variegations. Grass-like appearance to 18 inches. In zones 5 and colder, it should be wintered over indoors as a houseplant.

Butomus umbellatus (Flowering Rush)—Triangularly shaped, rushlike blades to 3 feet in height with umbels of pink flowers held above the leaves in mid to late summer. Does not do well in hot climates or in small pots, although it is among the slower to propagate. Hardy to Zone 3.

Water-sensitive plant,
Neptunia aquatica
Photo by Greg Speichert/Crystal Palace Perennials

Hairy pennywort,
Hydrocotyle ssp.
Photo by Greg Speichert/Crystal Palace Perennials

Flowering rush,
Butomus umbellatus
Photo by Greg Speichert/Crystal Palace Perennials

Water canna

Photo by Greg Speichert/Crystal
Palace Perennials

Calla palustris (Bog Arum)—A creeping rhizome bearing waxy green, heart-shaped leaves with small, white, occasional flowers followed by red berries; grows to only 8 inches. Full sun to slight shade. Hardy to Zone 4.

Canna ssp.—Tropical, lush-colored flowers in mid-to-late summer and elegant, broad, pointed leaves may be grown in 2 to 8 inches of water. Winter over indoors as houseplants in colder climates.

Carex stricta 'Bowles Golden' (Golden Sedge)—Commonly found in garden centers, this 16 inch high, clumping golden-leafed grass will grow with two inches of water over the plant's crown. Full sun to slight shade. Hardy to Zone 5.

Colocasia spp. (Taro or Elephant Ear)—Tropical, huge leaves of green or reddish casts may be grown in full sun in 2 to 4 inches of water over the plant crown. The bulbs need to be removed, dried, and rested over the winter.

Taro or elephant ear,
Colocasia sp.

Photo by Greg Speichert/Crystal Palace Perennials

Butterfly plant,
Asclepias incarnata

Photo by Greg Speichert/Crystal Palace Perennials

N. Lily Pons

Hybridized and photographed by
Perry D. Slocum

Glyceria maxima ssp. (Manna Grass)—
Available in variegated form, but tends to
revert to common green. Prevent this by
cutting out green stems. Grows to 2 feet
and is highly invasive. Fully hardy.

Iris laevigata (Japanese Water Iris)—Not
to be confused with *Iris ensata* (formerly
known as *Iris kaemferi*), this iris is fully
hardy and will grow to a good 2 feet with
2–4 inches of water over the plant crown.
Blooms late spring to early summer for 3–4
weeks, flowers short-lived, but blooming in
succession. A slightly shorter variegated
variety is available. Many new colors and
hybrids are available.

Iris pseudacorus (Yellow-flag Iris)—
European native, now naturalized in North
America. Blooms early-to-midsummer and
may grow to 3 feet or more. Variegated
form grows to 3 feet. Fully hardy.

Cyperus alternifolius (Umbrella Grass)—
Tropical, parasol-like umbels grow to 3½
feet; it can be wintered over in frost areas
either indoors as a houseplant or its pot
sunk below the ice level in the pond. Available in both dwarf and variegated forms.

**Iris versicolor,
'Mysterious Monique'**

Photo by Greg Speichert/Crystal
Palace Perennials

Iris versicolor (Blue-flag Iris)—Native to North America, this fully hardy species grows to 30 inches and is not so vigorous as the Yellow-flag species with narrow, purplish-blue petals. Fully hardy.

Juncus effusus spiralis (Corkscrew Rush)—Corkscrew-curling foliage may grow 12 inches long, but the plant tends to be rather prostrate by habit. Fully hardy.

Lobelia cardinalis (Cardinal Flower)—Grows to 30 inches with 1–4 inches of water over the plant crown, flowering in red spires in late summer. Some strains may be hardy to a zone 4, however, it is best considered tender even in zone 5.

Marsilea spp. (Water clovers)—Most forms of this floating-to-upright plant are tropical and can be grown as annuals in temperate zones. Generally, the variegated

Water clover, Marsilea ssp.

Photo by Greg Speichert/Crystal Palace Perennials

and marked forms are tropical. A common green form (M. *drumondii*) may be hardy through zone 5, especially if the plant is kept below the ice. Highly invasive.

Mentha aquatica (Water Mint)—A scrambling, purple-tinged leafed aromatic plant with dainty lilac flowers in mid-to-late summer. Highly invasive, broken bits or trailing runners will root throughout the pond. Hardy to Zone 4.

Menyanthes trifolia (Bog Bean)—Hardy, scrambling habit that is slow to establish, but then becomes rampant after 3 or 4 years. Prefers shallow areas and edges of the pond or bog garden; offers delicate, white fringed flowers in late spring to early summer along with its three-leafed foliage.

Myosotis palustris (Water Forget-me-not) A dainty plant growing to only 6 inches, it may be grown in 2–3 inches of water over the plant crown. Dainty blue flowers in early summer may set seed. Hardy through zone 5.

Myriophyllum aquaticum (Parrot's Feather)—A delightful plant that also functions as a submerged oxygenator. Its whorled, feathery, lime-green tips float at the water's surface. Must be wintered over beneath any ice in cold climates.

Cardinal flower, Lobelia cardinalis 'Red Giant'

Photo by Greg Speichert/Crystal Palace Perennials

**Parrot's feather,
Myriophyllum aquatica**

Photo by Greg Speichert/Crystal
Palace Perennials

**Variegated arrow
arum, Peltandra
virginica var.**

Photo by Greg Speichert/Crystal
Palace Perennials

**Water bluebell, Ruellia
brittonia**

Photo by Greg Speichert/Crystal
Palace Perennials

Orontium aquaticum (Golden Club)—
Grows to only 12 inches, and very slow to establish and bloom its unique white and yellow pencil-thin flowers in the early summer. This plant needs acid soil, and a roomy pot. It may be grown with 3–10 inches of water over the plant's crown. It is fully hardy in zone 5. Colder zones should winter it below any ice level.

Peltandra virginica (Arrow Arum)—
Slow growing to 2 feet, hardy aquatic with shiny, arrow-shaped leaves and a relatively inconspicuous white arum flower. A larger version growing to perhaps 3 feet above the water while planted 12–18 inches below can be found growing in North American wetlands. Seeds collected from these plants are easily propagated. A variegated form is available.

Pontederia cordata (Pickerel Weed)—
Shiny, spear-shaped leaves on fleshy stems produce spires of clustered purple-blue, white, or pink flowers in mid-to-late summer. Generously sized pots are recommended to accommodate the plant, which grows year-to-year leaving behind a large clump of dead rootstock. Because commercially supplied plants may not be fully hardy in colder zones, the plant should be wintered below any ice level.

Sagittaria ssp. (Arrowhead)—Available in both narrow-leafed and broad-leafed varieties and growing with 2–6 inches of water over the crown to 18–24 inches in height, this veined, arrow-shaped leafed plant produces branches of dainty white flowers in midsummer. Hardy to zone 4.

Saururus cernuus (Lizard's Tail)—Pale green heart-shaped leaves grow to 18 inches in 2–5 inches of water over the plant crown with clusters of white blooms in mid-to-late summer. When confined to a pot, the plant is not invasive. Hardy to zone 4.

Scirpus ssp. (Bulrushes)—Growing to 3–5 feet with 2–6 inches of water over the crown, bulrushes produce brown flowering tufts in midsummer. The common green form requires a broader-mouthed pot than the *S. albescens* (vertically striped cream and green) and the *S. zebrinus* (horizontally striped). Fully hardy.

Thalia dealbata (Hardy Water Canna)—Not nearly as lush in appearance as its name implies; growing to 6 feet with elongated leaves, the plant has bractlike, purplish flowers held above on tall stems. Even

in zone 5, the plant should be wintered below the ice to ensure its wintering over.

Typha ssp. (Cattails)—Fully hardy plant family, the *T. latifolia* form found growing in the wild is too tall and weighty for potting in the water garden. Varieties that will

**Pickerel weed,
Pontederia ssp.**

Photo by Greg Speichert/Crystal Palace Perennials

**Water parsnip,
Sium suave**

Photo by Greg Speichert/Crystal Palace Perennials

grow to 4 feet are *T. angustifolia*, *T. stenophylla*, *T. laxmanii*, and *T. minima*. *T. europa* or the micro-miniature cattail grows to only 18 inches with a fine, grass-like habit and very small pokers.

Zantedeschia aethiopica (Calla Lily)—Growing to 2 feet, huge, white arum flowers grace large, dark green, waxy leaves for 3–4 weeks in midsummer. The plant can be grown with 4–6 inches of water over the crown and should be wintered over well beneath any possible winter ice. Hardy to zone 5.

Submerged Aquatics

These plants are the key to maintaining clear water. They do need sunlight. If the water remains at 70°F or above in the summer months, many of them may display scraggly growth. Most are subject to fish-nibbling.

Cabomba ssp.—Appears as a smaller-scaled version of *myriophyllum*, growing to 8 inches. This plant will tolerate both shade and warmer waters. It is tenderly hardy below ice levels.

Ceratophyllum demersum (Hornwort or Coontail)—A bristly-looking, darkish green plant that floats free in the summer and anchors itself on the pond bottom during the dormant winter period. Hardy if below any ice.

Elodea ssp. (*densa* often sold as *anacharis*, commonly called Canadian pondweed)—The *canadensis* form has small leaves on brittle stems; the *densa* or *anacharis* form has longer leaves but is not as hardy. *Lagarosiphon major* is often sold as *elodea crispa* or *anacharis*, which has longer, dark green leaves that curl back on themselves as they grow along the long stems. One of the best for clear water, but can be extremely vigorous and needs control.

**Golden Buttons,
Cotula coronipilolia**

Photo by Greg Speichert/Crystal Palace Perennials

Eleocharis acicularis (Hairgrass)— Bright green, grassy plant that grows only 6–8 inches forming a carpet on a pond bottom prepared with sand or soil.

Myriophyllum ssp. (Milfoil)—Feathery foliage along long stems of various shades of darker greens. Can be established in deeper waters of 3 or 4 feet. Prone to filamentous algae. Not as efficient at nutrient removal as other plants, and highly invasive.

Potamogeton crispus (Curled Pondweed) Long, crinkled, thin leaves prove too vigorous a grower for the typical water garden. Fully hardy.

Sagittaria subulata forma natans— Grows to only 4–5 inches, appearing as a grassy turf. While it may colonize in any submerged potting, it is most effective established in a pea gravel or sandy bed over the entire pond bottom. This can be difficult to achieve if fish are present—they can uproot it as well as eat it. A very efficient plant.

Valisneria ssp. (Tape Grass)—A family of fine, long-bladed, oxygenating plants that grow to 2 feet or more. The *spiralis* form grows to only 6–8 inches. More tolerant of warmer waters than most of the above.

Floating Aquatics

These plants are not potted, but simply float freely on the water's surface. Their trailing roots, however, will root in available soil.

Azolla ssp. (Fairy Moss or Water Fern)— Small, fronded plantlets that turn reddish in full sun and in the cooling days of autumn. Can be so invasive they kill aquatics below trying to grow in the shade they produce. Goldfish will not eat this plant; it is usually controlled by netting out. It is killed by freezing, but some may winter over.

Eichhornia ssp. (Water Hyacinth)— Swollen, air-filled leaf bases give these tropical glossy plants buoyancy. They spread by plantlets produced from branchings of the mother plant and are highly invasive to the point of governmental regulation in their transport across state lines. Lovely lilac blooms last but a day.

Hydrocharis morsus-ranae (Frogbit)—A delightful, dainty plant of glossy, air-puffed leaflets that spread by runners. Tiny white flowers may be so inconspicuous as to not be noticed. Supposedly hardy by wintering over in turion form on the pond bottom, this rarely happens in the typical water garden.

Lemna ssp. (Duckweed)—The *minor* form is quite common and can return year after year. It seems to wane during the hot summer months and is usually controlled by fish nibblings. However, it can be highly invasive and require netting out. The tropical *major* form is two to three times larger and quite lush appearing. Fish do not favor this one; net out as needed for control. *L. trisulca* (ivy-leaf duckweed) is hardy and less invasive with tiny angular leaves that hang just below the water's surface. It is usually gobbled up by the fish and may become lost among the more vigorous family-members.

Pistia stratiotes (Water lettuce)—Spongy, lime-green, deeply creased leaves characterize this floating tropical plant. It spreads by branching plantlets from the mother plant.

Mimulus × 'Lothain Fire'
Photo by Greg Speichert/Crystal Palace Perennials

APPENDIX 3

Figuring Quantities of Building Supplies

CONCRETE BLOCKS

Crushed limestone (Hardcore) is sold by the ton. Also known as #53. One ton is approximately 20 cubic feet.

Flagstone, slate, and flat granite are sold by the ton. See chart below for individual coverage.

Ground cover aggregates and pea gravel are sold by the ton. Pebbles, nuggets, and chips are generally figured at 100 square feet of coverage at a depth of 2 inches or 150 square feet of coverage at a depth of 1½ inches.

Mulch, in the form of shredded bark, is sold by the yard, with one yard covering 100 square feet at a 3-inch depth.

Sand is sold by the ton. One ton is approximately 20 cubic feet.

Stone bark and crater rock ground cover aggregates give approximately 225 square feet of coverage per ton at a 2-inch depth.

Topsoil, pulverized, is sold by the ton/yard with 1 ton equal to about 1 yard. One ton/yard covers 27 cubic feet.

Type	Approx. Thickness	Approx. Coverage/Ton
Lannon Select	¾″ × 1¼″	100 sq. ft.
Lannon Regular	1½″ × 2½″	70 sq. ft.
Pennsylvania	¾″ × 1½″	150 sq. ft.
Tennessee	¾″ × 1½″	130 sq. ft.
Tennessee	1½″ × 2¼″	80 sq. ft.
Cherokee Marble	1¼″ × 1½″	100 sq. ft
Vermont Slate	¾″ × 1″	170 sq. ft.
North Carolina Granite	1½″ × 2″	70 sq. ft.

BOULDERS

Featherock weighs approximately 64 pounds per cubic foot.

Granite weighs approximately 200 pounds per cubic foot.

Marble weighs approximately 150 pounds per cubic foot.

Brick, new and used, is figured at 4.5 bricks per square foot, laid flat.

Cement and Mortar, sold by the 80 pound bag, premixed, will fill 2 square feet at a 4 inch depth.

Cobbles are round stones, usually fitting in two open hands. There are 30 to 35 per ton.

CALCULATING VOLUME OF CONCRETE

For squares and rectangles, multiply the thickness in inches × the length × the width and divide by 12 to get the number of cubic feet. Divide that by 27 to get the number of cubic yards.

For circles, multiply the thickness in inches × 3.14 × the radius squared (the radius × itself) and divide by 12 to get the number of cubic feet. Divide that by 27 to get the number of cubic yards needed.

PUMP SIZING CHART

LIFTS	1'	3'	5'	10'	15'	20'
	120	70				
	170	140	100			
GPH	205	168	120			
	300	255	205	70		
	325	300	270	130		
	500	435	337	210	65	
	600	580	517	414	230	90
	710	690	670	580	380	150
	810	790	745	613	415	173
	1200	1170	1100	1000	840	520
1/6HP				900	690	480
0.3HP				2750	1750	750
0.4HP				3250	2500	1550

COMPUTING SURFACE AREA OF POND

1. Rectangular shape: Multiply length × width.

2. Circular shape: Multiply 3.14 × radius squared (half diameter).

RECOMMENDED TUBING BORE FOR PUMPS TO WATERFALLS

½ inch diameter	for flows up to	120 GPH
¾ inch diameter	for flows up to	350 GPH
1 inch diameter	for flows up to	1000 GPH
1¼ inch diameter	for flows up to	1500 GPH
1½ inch diameter	for flows up to	3000 GPH

COMPUTING POOL VOLUME IN U.S. GALLONS

1. Mathematical formulas:
a. If computed in inches, divide the total by 231.
b. If computed in feet, multiply the total by 7.5.
Rectangular shapes: multiply length × width × depth.
Circular shapes: multiply 3.14 × radius squared × depth.
2. Using a domestic water meter: Use a wrench to turn the locking nut on the meter to remove the lid. Record the reading before filling the pool. Subtract this figure from the figure recorded after the filling is completed. No water should be used in the house during filling.
3. Using hose output: Fill a large bucket for exactly 60 seconds. Measure the water in pints and divide by 8 to compute U.S. gallons. Record the start and stop times of the pool filling. Multiply the total minutes required for filling by the number of gallons the hose discharges in one minute.

COMPUTING POOL VOLUME IN LITERS

1. Multiply length × width × depth in meters × 28.41 for rectangular volume.
2. Multiply depth in meters × metric radius squared × 20.75 for circular volume.

MATHEMATICS OF CONVERSIONS

To Convert	Multiply by	To Obtain
inches	2.54	centimeters
inches	25.4	millimeters
feet	30	centimeters
pounds	0.45	kilograms
U.S. gallons	3.8	liters

Fahrenheit to Celsius: Subtract 32, multiply by 5, divide by 9.

INDEX